S.O.S.

~ Songs Of Sobriety ~

A Personal Journey Of Recovery

There are many books out there dealing with the recovery process. We believe this is the first one to channel the process, the emotions, the healing, in linear story fashion, in the form of poetry. This journey of the first ten years of sobriety is expressed through the inspired verse of poet C.S. Blue.

S.O.S.

~ Songs Of Sobriety ~

A Personal Journey
Of Recovery

Poems by

C.S. BLUE

S.O.S.

~ Songs Of Sobriety ~

A Personal Journey Of Recovery

ISBN 0-9635499-3-6 / ISBN 978-0-9635499-3-8

Editor: Laura LeHew
Proofreader: Paulette Schreiner

Published by:

➤ ARROWCLOUD ➤
PRESS

for more information go to:
www.wordsongs.com

Dedication:

To my wife, Paulette, whose encouragement, dedication and assistance were invaluable in bringing this book to fruition.

I would also like to dedicate this book to all those who are on the path of recovery. May the journey bring you success and much joy.

I would like to thank you, H.P. (Higher Power), for the gift of my sobriety, the gift of this poetry, and for your continued grace in my life each day.

C.S. Blue

C.S. Blue won his first poetry award at age twelve. He started writing poetry seriously when he was eighteen. After various jobs in his youth, Steven began a career in stage production that would last 27 years. These experiences helped to shape his poetry and his dream of someday having his poems published.

Although Steven never stopped writing, it took many years of struggling with alcoholism, drug addiction, and a near-death experience to bring him back to his dream. With the help of some friends, he was able to get sober, slowly recover, and begin to put his life back together.

Steven has been sober for over 25 years now. During that time he has written many poems about sobriety and addiction, as well as the growth process of recovery. He organized many of those works into this book. We hope you enjoy sharing his journey. It is our wish that it may help and inspire you in your own life struggles.

Introduction:

This is the story of one man's struggle to be free. I am that man and this is my story; my struggle for sobriety and a new life that was promised me. A promise that came true.

It is a journey that is told through the poems I wrote. It is about the first 10 years of my recovery; struggling first to be clean and sober, then to stay in recovery and live a happy and fulfilling life.

It is my sincere hope that this book may help and inspire those of you who are struggling in recovery, addictions of any kind and life's troubles in general. It is a struggle of the brave, to be sure.

This book will be a revelation to some, an intervention for others. It is my sincere hope that you will find some inspiration within the poems themselves, on the lyrical journey of these pages. Living life on life's terms is what made it all possible.

May it aid you on your spiritual journey . . .
May peace be with you . . .

C.S. Blue

Forward:

This is the story of a man's recovery from a hopeless state of mind and body; from a hopeless dope fiend to a dopeless hope fiend.

A little bit about sobriety:

How do you explain the concept to someone who really needs help, that surrendering is winning, when they've been taught all their lives—never surrender! Winning is everything!

How can it be shown that you must surrender your will? That your own will is what got you here. Your best thinking; your best trying—**your will** . . . is what got you to this point of hopelessness, where you now find yourself.

You think you can control it. Yes . . . you may feel good for a couple of days when you've gone on the wagon, after remorseful drinking or using, or actions like threatening or hurting someone you love. So you stop drinking or using for a couple of days, or a few weeks and you feel good. You think you've got it under control: "See, it doesn't control me. I control it!" But before you know it, you're drinking and using again. You just can't win. How did this happen . . . again?

Because you've got to let go; to realize you're not in control. You've got to surrender your stubborn will! You may think that is a funny thing. You can't relate to losing. What you can't see, that just isn't funny—this disease can kill . . . and it will!

I know it sounds strange and alien; surrender to win . . . but it is how you begin; by admitting you are powerless. By accepting that someone else, a power greater than yourself, can help you. The willingness to reach out and let someone in, to help you, where you couldn't help yourself.

Sobriety—do you really want it? Can you really grasp it? You've got to really want it or you just won't get it. To stay clean, to stay sober, you've got to really want it for yourself, and you've got to surrender.

Surrender—Let go—Have Acceptance . . . that you can be helped, and you will be! For acceptance is the key, you'll see, if you let yourself be teachable.

— NOBODY ELSE CAN DO IT FOR YOU —
— YOU'VE GOT TO SURRENDER TO WIN —

It has been said that church is a place . . .
for those who do not want to go to hell
and that the fellowship of recovery is a place . . .
for those who have already been there.

Note: The thing that really scared me when I got sober was that I would not be able to write anymore or be creative. After so many years of getting high, I really believed that being high is what gave me my creative inspiration. I was so wrong! Since I've been sober I've been more creative, more inspired and more focused than ever, as this book will clearly show.

Also, at two years sober I had an epiphany. I realized that I had always been this creative person that I am, even as a child . . . many years before taking my first drink.

C.S. Blue

CONTENTS

POETRY

C.S. Blue
1955-2000

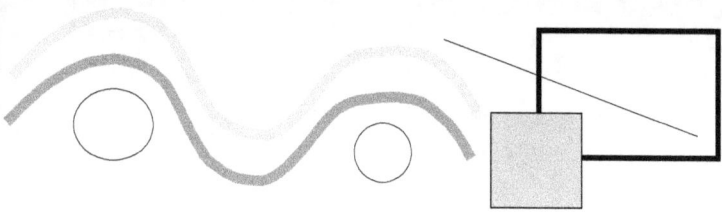

CHAPTER

1

PRELUDE TO SOBRIETY:

REACHING OUT, CRYING TO BE HEARD

Rebirth

Rebirth was very energetic,
Like a light beam or a sound beam,
Theoretically.
Moving along . . . zooming above the earth,
I knew I was there, yet I didn't know where.

To Life and to the earth . . .
Just a slim chord connected me.
I knew . . .
That if it broke I would be gone;

But for some reason I didn't care
And it was silent;
But somehow that silence
Was like sound . . . way up there.

Circling . . . circling . . . circling,
Around and around and around,
Knowing not . . . who I was
Or where I was bound;
But I knew I existed,
I knew I was there,
I knew I was going . . . somewhere.

Circling . . . circling . . . circling,
Around and around and around,
Then I landed—energetically,
Zap . . . zap . . . I hit the ground;

And looked around to see
—Astoundingly,
The light that was surrounding me.

Aboundingly, I knew
I had come home.

Electrically I stood,
As well as, you know, I could;

To walk along so free
And speak my thoughts to be:
To seek out life again
And—of course—get high again!
~~~~~~~~~~~~~~~~~~~~~
A little back story about this poem:

I wrote this poem after a near death experience of a drug
overdose in 1971.

I was left for dead, by other drugged out people, for about
two hours, but my wife stayed by my side. Eventually I
came back to consciousness.

When I awoke, it was as if I was being electrically charged
throughout my whole body. As I stood, I felt like a robot:
every fiber of my being was getting an electrical charge
as I started to move again.

It took me awhile to realize I was alive. It took me longer
to realize who I was and where I was. Everything came
back very slowly—and very electrically! It scared the crap
out of me!

The disease of alcoholism, be it drugs, alcohol, or a
combination thereof, is a very strong master. It would be
16 more years before I would get clean and sober.

So join me now . . .
on my journey to recovery.

3

The Barroom Blues

Standing here
At the end of the bar,
Wine glass in my hand.
My eyes are red
And you can see their sadness,
But I just don't understand.

Why won't you come over
And talk to me?
I want to be a part of you
(You all seem so happy)
But I just don't know
What to do.

I've got these silent, withdrawn,
Barroom blues
      Again.
Don't know how I can
Go on anymore.
I think it's the end.

I've got these silent, withdrawn,
Barroom blues
      Once again.
No matter what happens,
It seems like
I just can't win.

Why am I alone
At the end of the bar?
Think I'll have another shot!
Then maybe you'll think
I'm good enough,
'Cause I sure want what you've got.

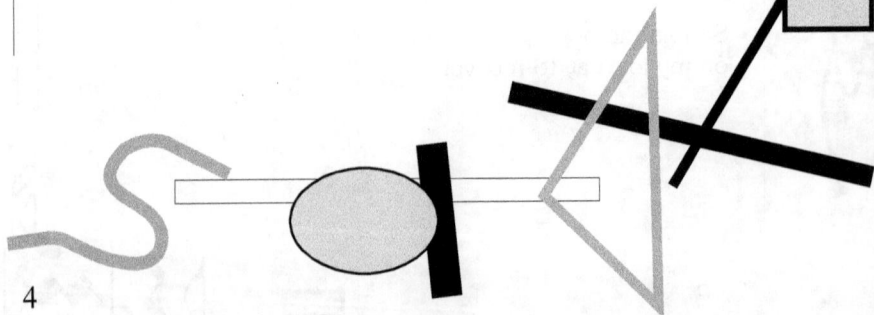

Why can't I just
Quit this drinkin'
And get on with my life?
Where is *mine*—where is *she*—
And why is everything screwed up
In my life?

I've got these silent, withdrawn,
Barroom blues
             Again.
Don't know how I can
Go on anymore.
I think it's the end.

I've got these silent, withdrawn
Barroom blues
             Once again.
No matter what happens,
It seems like
I just can't win.

Out Of Control Zone

Time is rare
and friends are few.
Where has it gone to
and where has it taken you?
Magic . . .
soothes your troubled soul.
But where is the . . . control?

Don't ever forget the dreamers;
but watch out, take care, beware
of bright-eyed schemers;
greedy . . . seedy . . . to the max
—their pacts.
No parcels full of caring
for the sharing of your soul.
Oh where is the . . . control?

Scraping the sand
off the bottom.
Following tracks:
long forgotten
footsteps erased from time.
Once again you find them
and bare your soul.
But where is your . . . control?

Miracles in the distance
call out to you.
It's time to light
the perspective view
of the endless new.

Followed the tracks through the years;
seen the highs, the lows, and the tears,
overcome the fears;
and magic . . .
soothes your troubled soul.
But where is your . . . control?

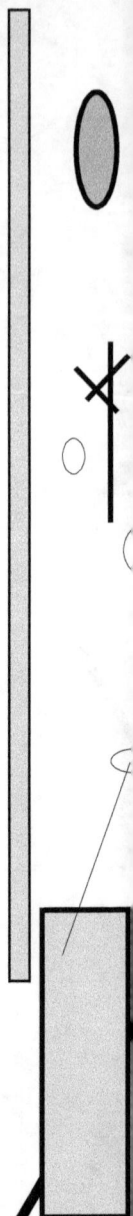

The waves know it,
for they calm when you sing.
The sun knows it,
for it shines when it sees you.
Don't get caught in the cycle.
Don't forget love
        is the key.
There are so many bumps
on this cross-track blues road
to finding your soul.
Oh where is the . . . control?

Why do you dwell
on dogma? . . .
cautioned by the wind
        to share,
                to care.

Is the sparkle
burnt to the crisp
in the wisp of time?
Did you forget
how to shine,
or will the business grin
just begin again?
Oh where is the . . . control?

Save it for the savior!
Save it for your child!
Can you be wild and still be true?
Is it still inside of you?
Anonymous affinities
pay the dues
for your blues.

Show them you can feel
what is real again,
and believe you still can
see your dreams.
For the schemer
always schemes,
and the dreamer
always dreams,
and the magic . . .
soothes your troubled soul.
But where is the . . . control?

Integral parts
start to share.
Musical sparks
make you aware,
daring . . . to care;
for the sign of the times
is in the air.
Patch it up—
like the seams in your dreams
and find your . . . control.

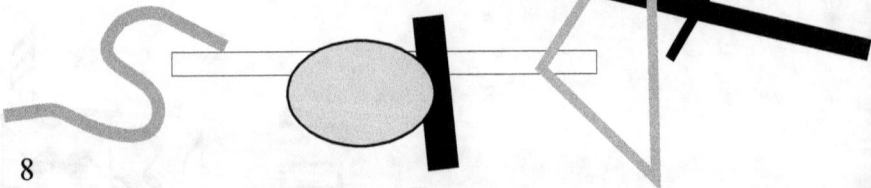

My Plea

Try as you may,
it's hard to hold back
when you're stuck.
If you lose it,
what's gonna happen
to the brighter day?

You've got to hold on
to what you believe.
Don't try to get even,
because things
take their own course, of course.
It's gonna happen anyway.
Try to take it day-to-day.

Help me . . . ouch!

The force of spirit
that you are,
come here from afar.
I know the way I feel;
have faith in who you are.

I'm sore—
I wanna shine;
but my time
doesn't seem to align
with Nature's rhyme . . . anymore.
    Anyway,
      which way shall I go?

Help me . . . out!

Man . . . Without A Band

you know . . .
i thought this was my home
but i guess it's not anymore
maybe i don't belong anywhere
maybe only on these pages

just a blob of ink
spilling out my emotions
where it doesn't matter
if anyone listens or not
if anyone cares

what's the point
nothing matters—
empty words on a page
filled with someone's blather

just you
alone as you came
alone as you go
no one *new* . . .
no one will know

maybe keeping it
          serene
doesn't mean a thing
maybe it's all so . . . temporary
          anyhow
and life's grass will just grow
          over you
like a bunch of weeds
that no one bothered to cut
you'll rot away
          unnoticed . . .

just another part
of the brown . . . hard . . . dirt
        ground underfoot
or burned into soot
—blown on the breeze
to another place of . . . dis-ease
        it doesn't matter
no one will notice that
        either

it makes no difference
'cause who's gonna pay
to see it your way?
not a damn soul
—i'm outta control
rolling down a crooked hill
bangin' into rocks
in my dirty socks and jeans

no means to my chatter
don't know what's a'matter
'cept i feel like home made shit
that someone just spit

get over it
stop the run
it's no longer fun
        you're done
'cause if you don't
you'll just end up floatin'
face down in the never lands
singin' a song of grimy hands
'cause you're just a man . . .
without a band!

Green Trees

God . . .
Life . . .
We two . . .
Our experiences . . .
Everything about us!

Just for once
to shine with the sun.
Just for the reaction;
      a fraction
      of satisfaction.

As if you cared
green trees for me.
Blue skies cry,
wonder why?
As if you cared!

Just for the dance
that has begun.
Just for the caring;
      the awareness
      of the sharing.

Just for a chance
not to run.
Just to be true;
      a small clue
      of what to do.

As if you cared
green trees for me.
Blue skies cry,
wonder why?
As if you cared!

Alone Again Or

Conversion of soul cleaning time,
the cobwebs scream in rhyme,
for the rhythm of the smoke signal key
        in your memory.

Sittin' here
alone again or
just makin' it with my memories?

Just sittin' here
alone again . . .
makin' it with my memories.

Guitar strings stretch for miles . . .
It's awhile before they call
—stalls of horses.
The courses you have to follow
seem so oak tree hollow
        in your memory.

Sittin' here
alone again or
just makin' it with my memories?

Just sittin' here
alone again . . .
makin' it with my memories.

You're flying in the fire,
pleased with desire,
but the easel to the artist
is just a place to make a stand.

        Your time is at hand!

Chair Dreams

Sitting in my chair
Starin' out my window
Dreaming about all the things
I'm gonna do . . . and see . . . and be

You're gonna love me
And it's going to be the best love ever
If I can just get out of this chair
And get it together

Chair dreams
Take me here and there
Chair dreams
Take me everywhere
Chair dreams
Seem so crystal clear
      For a moment
But then they're gone . . . again
And it's just another chair dream

I know . .
I was gonna have a hit song
And a house in the country
Sit in a rocker on my front porch
With endless inspiration

I know . . .
I was gonna paint my masterpiece
Write a prize-winning novel
And I remember . . .
Sometimes when I'm high enough

But I just can't seem
To get out of this chair
Can't seem to get motivated
To go anywhere

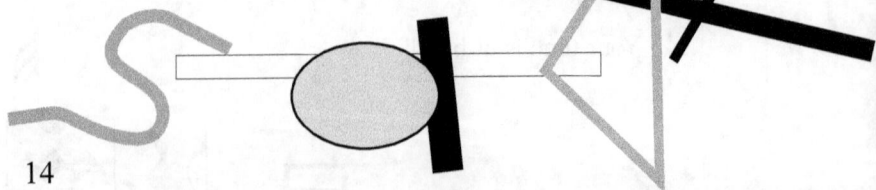

And my dreams slip away
(To the back of my mind)
Till another day
When the right combination finds
My chair dreams

Chair dreams
Take me here and there
Chair dreams
Take me everywhere
Chair dreams
Seem so crystal clear
        For a moment
But then they're gone . . . again
It's just another chair dream

You're gonna love me
And it's going to be the best love ever
If I can just get out of this chair
And get it together

Chair dreams
Take me here and there
Chair dreams
Take me everywhere

Chair dreams . . .
TAKE ME OUTTA HERE

Chair dreams . . .
        Seem so crystal clear
                For a moment
                        But then *I'm* gone again

It's just another chair dream

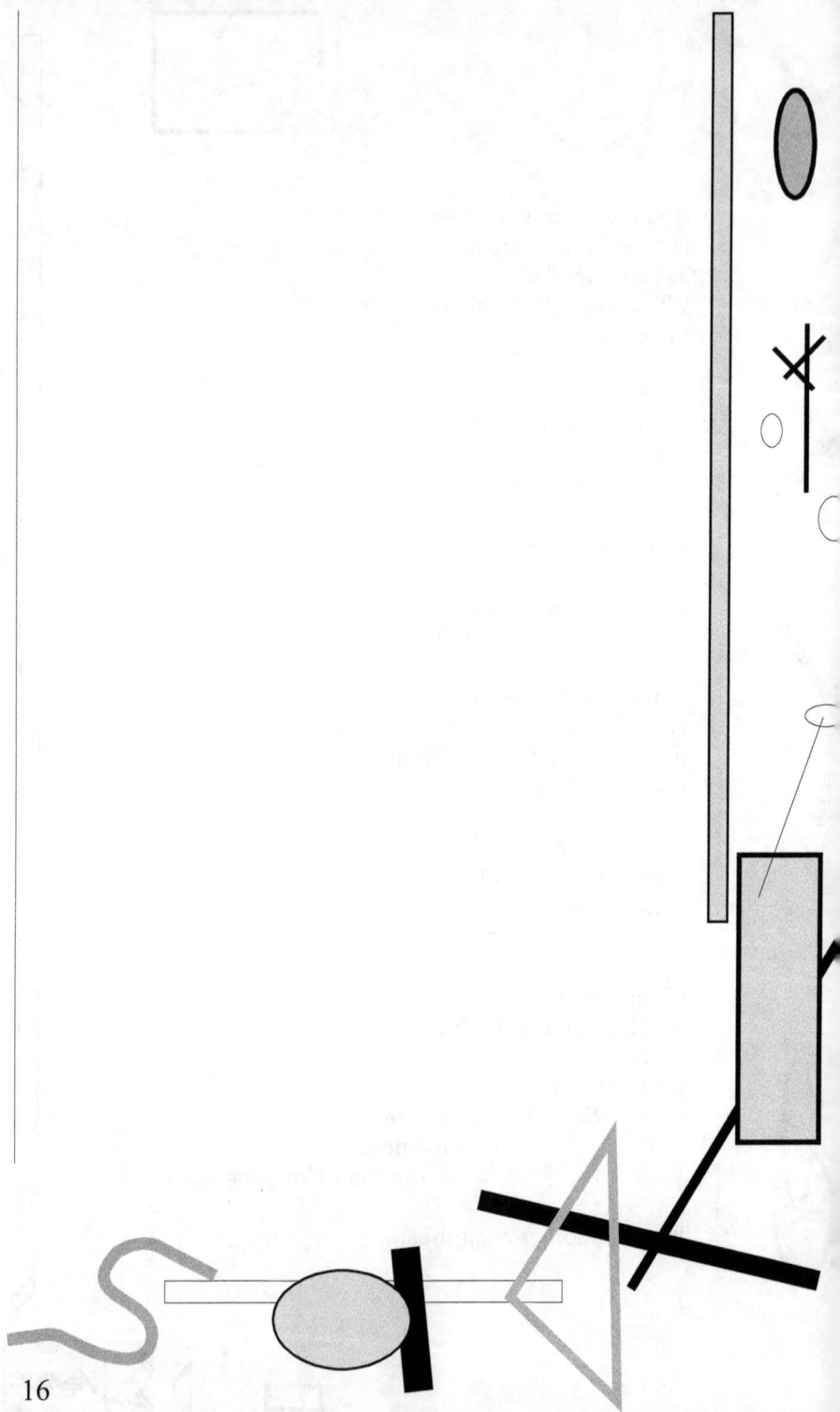

CHAPTER

2

THE FIRST 6 MONTHS:

NEWCOMER—WOW!

(WHAT A REVELATION)

Relief

I have
a renewed enthusiasm
for living,
for I have found
a spiritual guide
which gives my life
purpose and meaning
         again.

It is my own
as I understand it.
It comes from inside.

Although I don't always
recognize or listen
         to it,
I am grateful
to this guide.

To look forward
to this day's events
is irreplaceable.

Untitled

Grab the moment
Stake a claim
Strike a match
Place the flame
Pull back your arrow
Take good aim
And let it fly—>

High . . . higher
In your mind's eye
Soaring in the heights
Of your dreams
From sea to shining . . .
       See

Freak Doubt

Artificial frameworks
      Of anti-wisdom stimulants
            Are gone from me now.

Don't want no more
      Artificial brain drain
            Freak doubt!

19

What I See

It's been too long
since I've written or meditated.
My peace of mind is sorely lacking
and my patience is wearing thin.
So I'll try it again.

I know I must do
the footwork,
but stay out of the results.
It's only a daily reprieve (I remember),
contingent upon a spiritual way of life.
That is love . . . the action kind.

So I let go—
        to surrender
        to be quiet
        to realize
I am not in control . . .
and it's okay

to let something greater
guide me.
It sets my mind free;
to get back to that peace
inside me
where my faith, my hope
        and your grace
                are what I see.

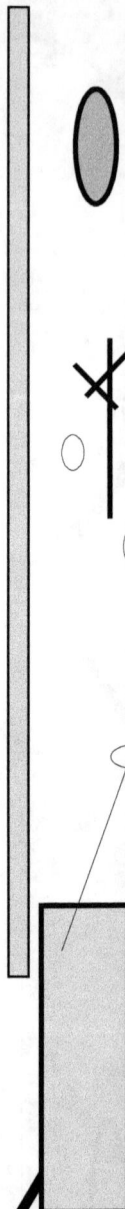

20

Thank You H.P.

I just want to thank you
For giving my life a lift
For the peace that's inside
And the light that I see

Thank you Higher Power
For giving me my gift
Thank you H.P.
For that feeling in me

I ask you each morning
Because it's not finished yet
And I thank you each night
So I'll never forget

You keep the strength up inside me
When things all seem wrong
With you here beside me
I know I belong

And I just want to thank you
For giving my life a lift
For the love that's inside
And the light that I see

Thank you Higher Power
For giving me my gift
Thank you H.P.
For that feeling in me

When I'm angry . . . confused . . . or just hurt
You are there
And the strength that you give
Helps me get up and share

When I think I am lost
You show me I'm found
When I think there is no one
You're always around

I just want to thank you
For giving my life a lift
For the peace that's inside
And the light that I see

Thank you Higher Power
For giving me my gift
Thank you H.P.
For that feeling in me

Oh How You Guide Me

In the fellowship around me,
it never ceases to astound me
how your message comes across
      loud and clear,
and all I have to do to find it
      is stay here;

to be reminded day by day,
there is a way for those like me
      to go.

And I know,
or I've made a decision
and come to believe . . .

Oh how you guide me.
Thank you for staying beside me.
The need to hide is leaving
      day by day.
I'm finding a way
      to live
in the gifts you give.

Sometimes,
when I think I'm losing
      it all,
you show me I am winning.
I see it come full circle
      once again.

What more can I say,
but to thank you each day,
for showing me the way
      to go.

23

And I know,
or I've made a decision
and come to believe . . .

Oh how you guide me.
Thank you for staying beside me.
The need to hide is leaving
        day by day.
I'm finding a way
        to live
in the gifts you give.

Oh how you guide me.
Thank you for staying beside me.
The need to hide is leaving
        day by day.
I'm finding a way
        to live
in the *freedom* you give.

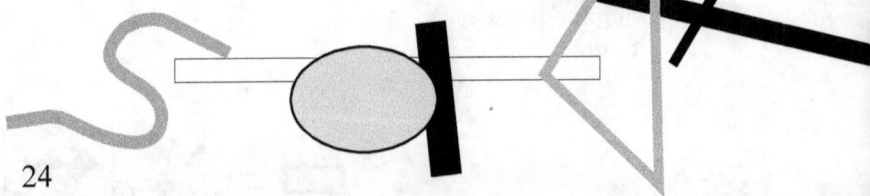

Brighter Day

Why do I feel
So full of love
Yet no one seems
To want it

I have so much
Inside to give
Why won't someone
Take it

I hunger
For that brighter day
When I wake up
Beside you

To hear you say
You'll stay . . .
I've been waiting so long
For that brighter day

I'm not afraid
To love
Though I've had my share
Of being let down

But where's the one
Who shares my faith
The one who's not scared
To stick around

I know it's been said
In better ways
But don't you know
I need you

Yet every time
I feel I'm close
Seems I can't get anywhere
Near you

Why do I feel
So full of love
Yet no one seems
To want it

I have so much
Inside to give
Why won't someone
Take it

I hunger
For that brighter day
When I wake up
Beside you

To hear you say
You'll stay . . .
I've been waiting so long
For that brighter day

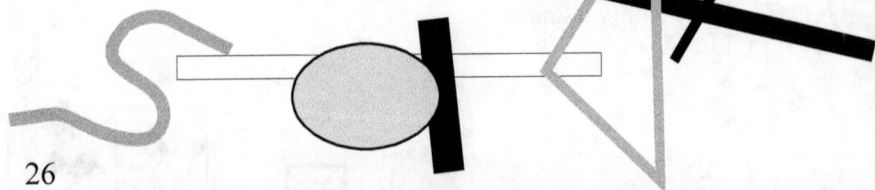

Lost In Motion

All my life
I've been misunderstood.
I'd fill you with inspiration
if I could.

Do you wonder why?

In the wind chimes of time
you are not a lost notion,
but maybe a notion
. . . lost in motion.

Do I hear a sigh?

I find humour
in the oddest places.
Tears of happiness
cover many faces.

Could a grown man cry?

Your Grace

I'm not writing or feeling
my spirituality
so much right now.

As soon as I have
the willingness
to get quiet and surrender,
you give me these words
to help me begin again.

When I pray . . .
It is not so much for the receiving
of things (I pray for)
as it is for the peace I get
from the quiet time of prayer;
my efforts to be closer
to you, H.P.

And the more I understand
your grace in my daily life,
the stronger the spiritual vision
becomes in me.

And the more I accept
your grace,
the stronger is your power
to set me free.

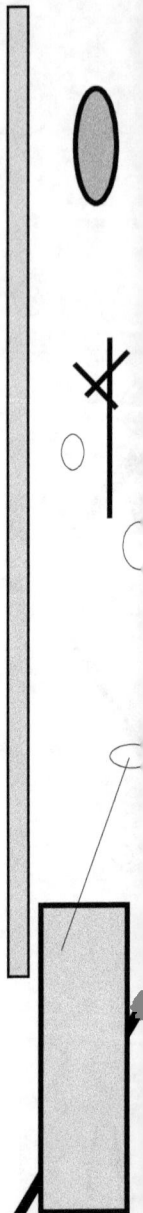

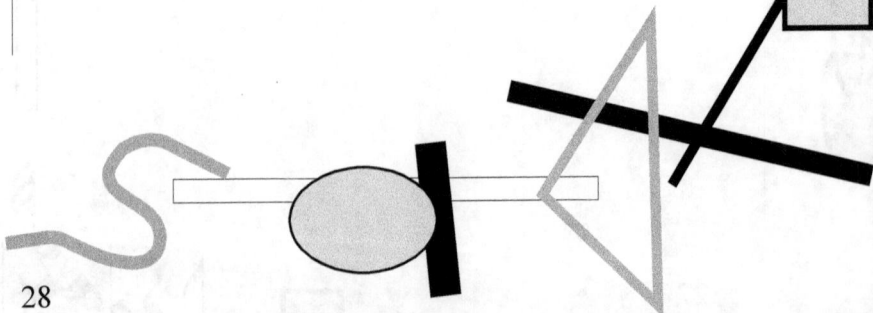

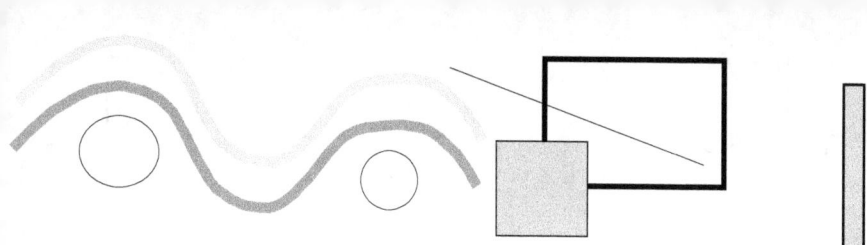

CHAPTER

3

6 MONTHS TO 1 YEAR:

THE STRUGGLE TO LIVE LIFE SOBER

All You've Got

Time flies by
When you're trying to live your dreams
And there's never enough time
It seems . . .
Every obstacle
Tries to get in your way
While you're trying to make it
To a better day

Well don't give up
It may not sound like a lot
But don't give up
Your dreams are all you've got
And some day . . .
You're gonna break right through
All the good (you've done)
Will come back to you

They say life is for living
Whatever you choose
But you've got to eke out
An existence
Unless you are born
Of the privileged few
You always will meet
With resistance

They say love is for giving
Without thought of reward
Well you've got to surrender
To win
Unless you realize
You are not in control
You know you have yet
To begin

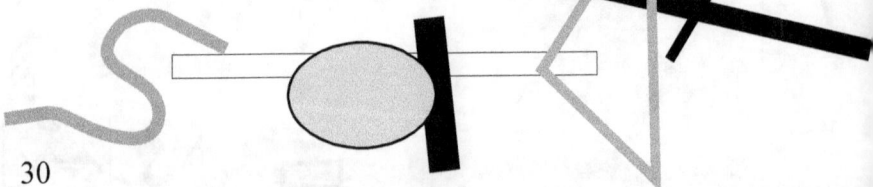

And don't give up
It may not sound like a lot
Don't give up
Your dreams are all you've got
And some day . . .
You're gonna break right through
All the good (you've done)
Will come back to you

Three Forty Four

It's three forty four
and the dealer's knockin' at my door.
Go away—please now,
and set my mind at ease.

I've felt that pain many times before.
I don't want to feel it anymore,
so go away—please, dealer,
leave me alone.

Lord help me!
Don't let me answer!
I'm so vulnerable
right now.

I want to shut out
the pain inside
and the dealer knows
just how.

Please, oh God,
make the knockin' go away.
I like the way I *feel* life now;
it's getting better day by day.

I feel so alone right now.
Stay by my side.
That old pain came back today.
I broke down and cried.

Tears welled up in me.
Resentments were felt.
But it's still not as bad
as when the dealer dealt.

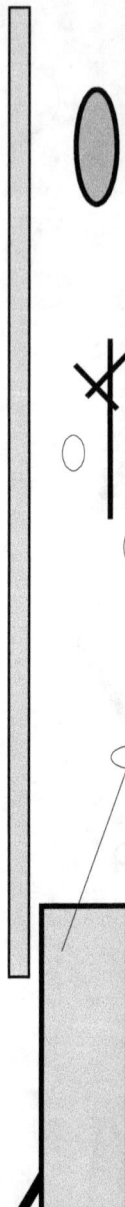

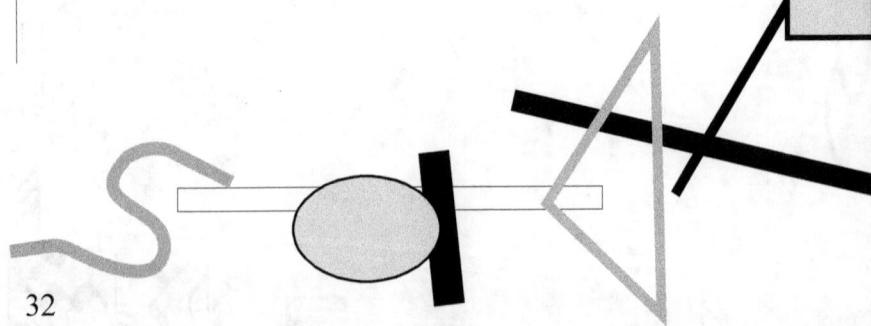

So help me walk through
this pain once more;
so I won't have to wake up
with my face on the floor.

It's three forty four
and the dealer's knockin' at my door.
Go away—please,
and set my mind at ease.

I don't want to score!
I don't want to be sore!
I don't want you no more—for sure!
And it's three forty four.
~~~~~~~~~~~~~~~~~
Note: This poem is based on an actual event that happened
to me at about six months sober. I wrote the poem right
after it occurred.

Turn It Over

When you're down
And the world seems wrong
When you feel
Like you don't belong
When it seems
That there's no way out
And you need to know
What it's all about

Turn it over
To someone who understands
Turn it over
To the one who guides your hands
Turn it over
With a little shove
Turn it over to love

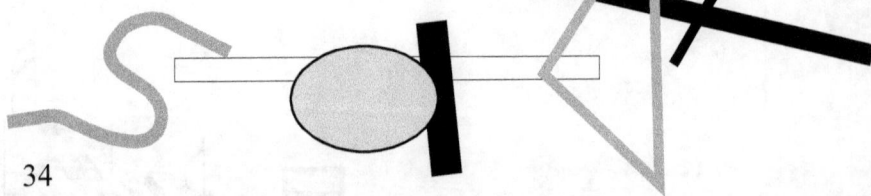

When it's all gone
And you don't know why
And you need someone
But you want to cry
And you want to reach out
But you just can't try
So all you can think is
You want to die

Turn it over
To someone who understands
Turn it over
To the one who guides your hands
Turn it over
With a little shove
Turn it over to love

When you're all alone
No one seems to care
And you want to know
Is there anybody out there?
'Cause it seems
That no one is like you
And you just don't know
What there is you can do

Turn it over
To someone who understands
Turn it over
To the one who guides your hands
Turn it over
With a little shove
Turn it over to love

When it's so confusing
And you want to rearrange it
But you know inside
You just can't change it
And you feel your back
Is up against the wall
And the ladder you've climbed
Is a long way to fall

Turn it over
To someone who understands
Turn it over
To the one who guides your hands
Turn it over
—Here's a little shove
Turn it over to love

35

The One Inside

the purity
      of your blessing
            defines me

reminds me
      of the child
            i used to be

the one inside
      still there
            to see

i only need ask
      by letting go
            of me

...aaAAhhHH CHOO!

What you give

is your sign

of relief,

not . . .

what you receive;

for it has

its own sense

of gratification;

just like a sneeze.

Footsteps

subtle secrets
        divide you
                simple solutions
                        guide you
                                adolescent attitudes
                                        adjust to
                                moral attributes
                        attuning
                your attention
        acknowledging
your actions
        following
                in footsteps
                        of deferential
                                decisions
                                        democratic
                                                direction
                                        daily doses
                                of doing
                        aligns
                anxious
        aching
away from
        anger
                hearing
                        heartfelt
                                honesty
                                        humbly
                                                heals
                                        the hurt
                                learning
                        loving
                lessons
        shows
you're surely
        shining

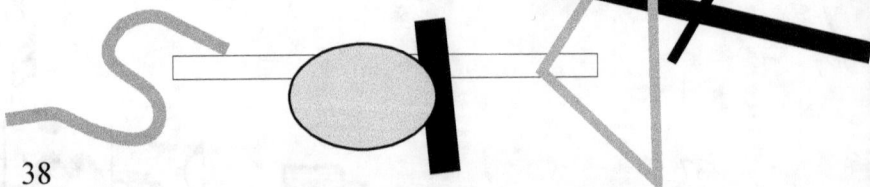

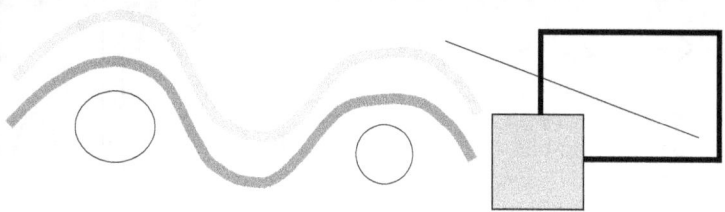

heading
for home
happy
softly
singing
in subtle
solitude
waiting
for wishes
wanting
for nothing
in worldy
wonder

Hard Knocks

Secondary flicks of the mind
Justification beyond the blind
Shooting star bright for a brief streak
A glimpse of the future takes a peek

Sacrifice for the love of another
A simple sign of purity
Like a financial windfall
It could be a sign of security

Some things, though taken away
Bring back to you so much more
A feeling of belonging
Like you never knew before

You're reaching and you're teaching
To see the fruit of the labor of love
As well . . . you're earning the love you're yearning for
As you're learning to become a part of

Helping someone
Helps you too
Hard knocks . . . get it through to you
Glimpses . . . from out of the blue

Secondary flicks of the mind
Justification beyond the blind
Shooting star bright for a brief streak
A glimpse of the future takes a peek

Your Troubled Mind

wake up
        wake up
your inner self
take it off the shelf
and live

make up
        make up
your troubled mind
there is so much
you have to give

aspire (to yourself)
for change
because
it's an inside job

don't let obstacles
set you back
your inner power
will guide you along

get healthy
by following your dreams
get strong
by knowing you belong

and how do you know
        by growing
take a risk
and persevere

41

wake up
        wake up
your inner self
take it off the shelf
and live

make up
        make up
your troubled mind
there is so much
you have to give

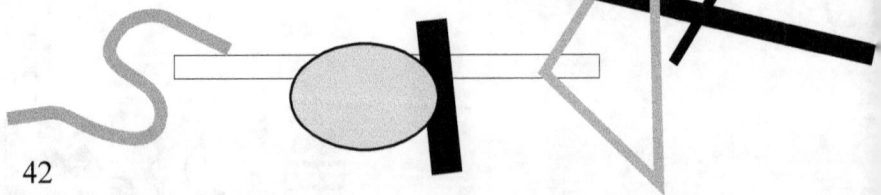

Fellowship By The River

days of drifting
desert breeze
basking in serenity

sunshine
sets my mind at ease
silver hearts fly free

swirling . . . shimmering
floating out of sight
begin their journey in the light

narrowly escaping
to the mountains in the distance
following the path of least resistance

glad I'm here
in acres of fun
bodies browning in the sun

morning ferry
slides into its slip
return run . . . one minute river trip

I'm well . . . red
it's semi . . . cool
down by the *Riverside* swimming pool

days of drifting
desert breeze
basking in serenity
~~~~~~~~~~~~~
Written at *The Fellowship By The River* sober retreat
in Laughlin, Nevada, at the Riverside Resort -
May, 1988, at 7 months sober.

Collective Individualism:
Once In A Blue Moon

Once in a blue moon
Comes a reason
Come on . . . join in
It won't be treason
The poison in your life
Be gone
Carry on

In collective individualism

Once in a blue moon
You can tell
Choose . . . to return
From a living hell
Now . . . is the moment
To be strong
Carry on

In collective individualism

A wave washes over me
Where the hell have I been
I feel . . .
And now I see
It's time
To cash my resentment chips in
It's time my ship came in
It's time to live again

Once in a blue moon
Hear the call
How . . . in heaven
Did I fall

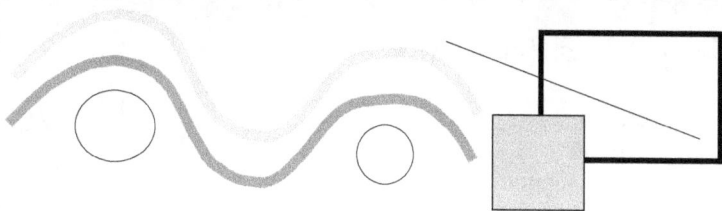

Now recall . . .
It's time to belong
Carry on

In collective individualism

Feeling sucked in by the current
Surrender to be free
Rise up to yourself again
Naturally

Once in a blue moon
Come what may
You . . . can recover
Day by day
Dreams do come true
It won't be long
Just remember
To be strong
And carry on

In collective individualism
~~~~~~~~~~~~~~~~~
Written at *The Fellowship By The River* sober retreat
in Laughlin, Nevada, at the Riverside Resort -
May, 1988, at 7 months sober.

45

Morning Meditation

Daily morning routine
of meditation moments:
peaceful interludes of silence
broken softly (at times);

by the late summer pecking
of scattered birds,
back again to build this year's nest
in my attic;

by the regular
(though intermittent)
low pitched howling
of the lonely dog next door;

by the subtle rhythm,
the far away whack
from the carpenter on the next block,
        building;

by the occasional airplane
shooting through the morning air,
for I am airport close . . .
(with one on both sides of me).

But for the most part
        it is quiet
during my twenty minutes or so
of morning time self-relaxation.

Sometimes . . .
plunk, the mail drops through my door,
although the postman
hasn't been early as of late.

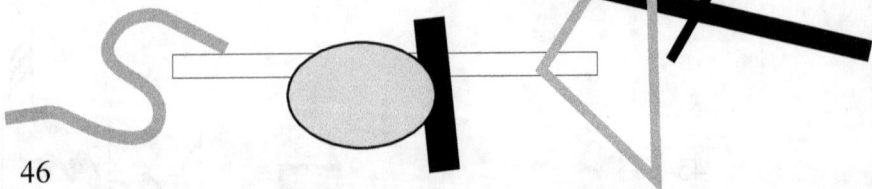

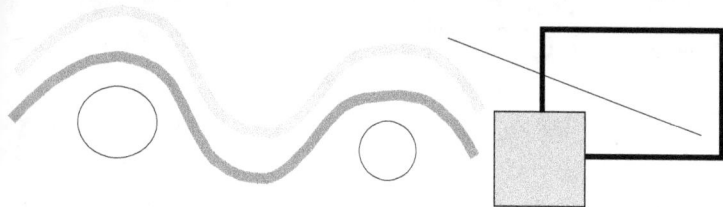

Sometimes . . .
no matter how I try to clear my thoughts,
sounds appear and I resign,
coming out a bit.

But I love these early morning sounds,
made acutely aware by my meditation;
although I am really far away,
lost in the depths of it.

The Nearest Of All

The colors of life
in the wildest array,
in all creatures
large or small,

although you seem
the farthest away,
really you are
the nearest of all.

I'm talking about someone
who helps me each day,
someone who guides me,
shows me the way.

You help me climb down
from my loneliness shelf.
You are a power . . .
greater than myself.

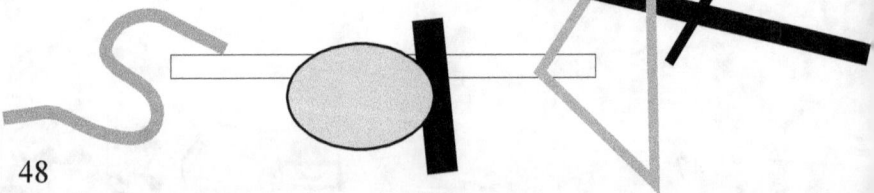

CHAPTER

4

YEAR 2:

FEELINGS— WHAT ARE THEY?

It's A Feeling

If it's right at the time that you feel it,
which it is,
then it's a feeling;
you know you can't steal it.

It's a feeling—must be given,
but cannot be given right,
unless you feel that it is right
at the time you feel it.

but then . . .
who reacts on these,
I say who goes
on these first feelings?

It's a feeling—must be given,
but cannot be given right,
unless you give it
at the time you feel it's right.

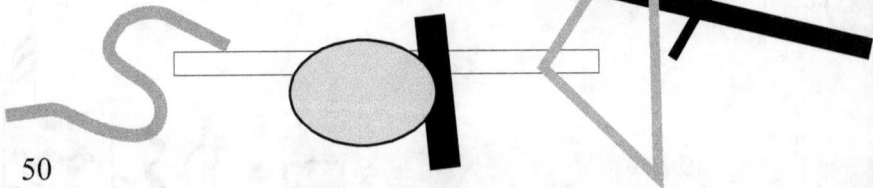

If The Feeling Is Real

It's not that we're different.
How can it be?
It's just that we care more now,
can't you see?

If the feeling is real
then it's one to believe,
that we all perceive what is real
if we feel it's our way
then we'll make it someday!

And it's here,
        it's right now.
I must show you,
        but how?
You must pick up on something
much closer
        right now . . .

Just to see you,
just to be with you,
if you know this feeling
then it all will work out.

I just want you together!
We all must come now.
Yes, where love sticks together,
it's here and here's how
it will stand as it stood;
but the love's deeper now.

And I don't even know
if the time is right now,
but it's just that I'm feeling
        so feeling . . .
                somehow.

Is It Enough

Is it enough
That it seems so confusing
Is it enough
That it hurts when you're losing
Is it enough
That you feel so alone
Is it enough

Is it enough
That her love you can't keep
Is it enough
That you can't get to sleep
Is it enough
That you want to go home
Is it enough

Is it enough
That it's hard when you fall
Is it enough
That you just want to crawl
Is it enough
That it all seems so cold
Is it enough

Is it enough
That you just feel abandoned
Is it enough
That you feel like you're stranded
Is it enough
That you're just feeling old
Is it enough

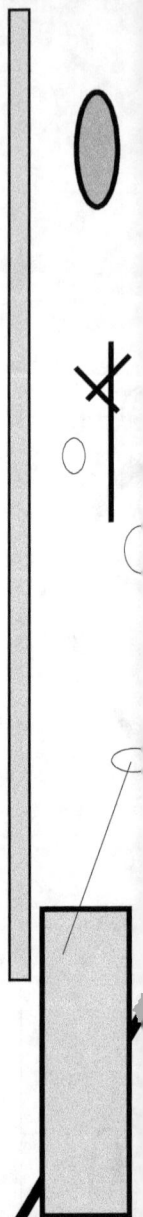

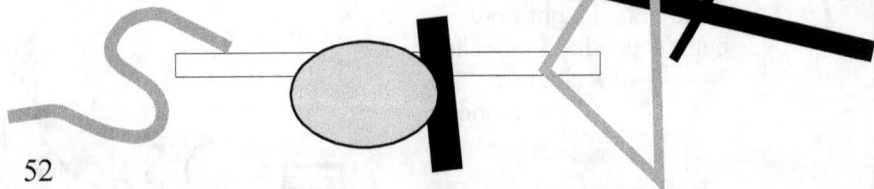

Brand New Day

You wait for her to come
But she can't wait to go
You want to help her make it
But she wants to steal the show

Your head is pounding
Your legs ache too
Can't stand the feeling
That she doesn't need you

Don't it make you wanna run
Don't it make you wanna sail away
Don't it make you hunger
For a brand new day

Your heart starts thumping
When she calls you again
You pace the floor, watch the door
To let her in

It's then you remember
She may not come around
It seems that when you need her
She never can be found

You're bound again to wonder why
Like so many other days
Deep inside you feel like cryin'
Don't it make you crazy

Don't it make you wanna run
Don't it make you wanna sail away
Don't it make you hunger
For a brand new day

You've got to let her go now
Take care of yourself
Got to take your love for her
Put it on a shelf

'Cause who is going to fulfill your needs
Who's gonna take care of you
No one is gonna really love you
Unless you do

Don't it make you wanna run
Don't it make you wanna sail away
Don't it make you hunger
For a brand new day

When it's over
And you're all alone
You've got to get up
And carry on

Take a stand where you are
Start to live like you mean it
Pretend you see the sunshine
Until you really see it

Though you can't figure out
What all the pain is for
The waves break on the shore (once more)
And morning is at your door

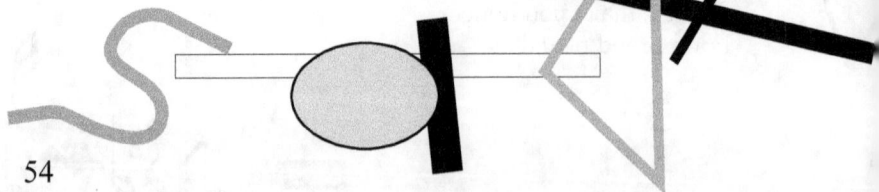

Wrenching

un-nurtured
unending
pain

what is pertinent
to the inner sanctum
of harmony

certainly not this

what do you read
what do you hear
what do you need
to make a clear-headed think

shrinking violets
in the night
do not shine

one more light
in your mind
sparks an inner drive
towards a goal
of nurturing

un-nurtured
unending
boredom
must end
to begin with

think about
what you think
analyze
what you see

don't get lost
in a sea of images

the picture is quite clear
you have got to start here
to make some sense
out of the wrenching

un-nurtured
unending
pain

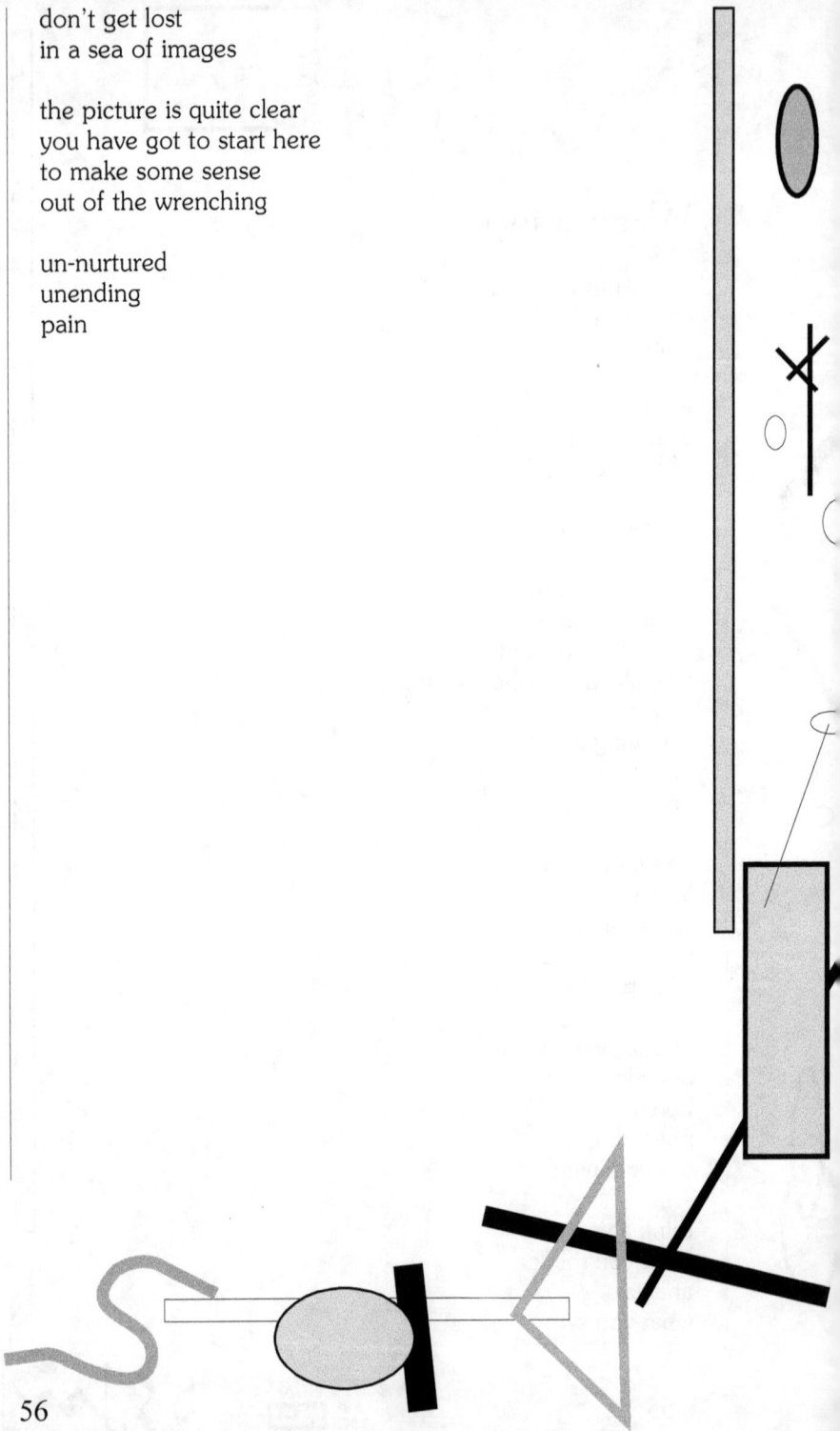

I Don't Wanna Be Here

Your head is full of anger again
and you don't know why.
It's like you never got
your first,
yet someone just snatched
the last piece of pie.

You're stuck
and you want to move,
can't seem to go anywhere.
All you can do
is pound your fist
and stare

out the window
(far away)
then that similiar feeling comes over you
just like those other days
when all you could say
            was . . .

get me outta here
—right now.
I don't wanna be here.
Can't you see?
Isn't it clear?
I wanna be gone.

Get me outta here
—right now.
I don't wanna be here.
Can't you see?
Isn't it clear?
I wanna be gone.

57

Your heart is full of pain again,
feels like you've come undone.
(Seems like) every time
you trust someone,
they take your heart and run.

You're hurt
and you wanna cry,
but the tears won't come (to bear).
All you can do
is grit your teeth and stare

out the window
(far away)
and that familiar feeling comes over you
just like that (long ago) day
when all you could say
           was . . .

get me outta here
—right now.
I don't wanna be here.
Can't you see?
Isn't it clear?
I wanna be gone.

Get me outta here
—right now.
I don't wanna be here.
Can't you see?
Isn't it clear?
I wanna be gone.

At work, I feel like I'm
the invisible man:
can't seem to get any attention.

You look right past me.
My hard working efforts
don't get any mention.

Can't (seem to) get anyone to help me,
to slow down long enough to see . . .
that I've got some good ideas,
but there's got to be room
        for me to be me.

And the whole world's asleep
in front of T.V.,
believing all the crap
that's thrown at them.

In the name of the dollar,
in the name of greed,
they believe competition
is the only way to win.

It's the unobtainable.
Isn't it strange?
It seems like everyone's
playing the game
that's really insane.

Once you have seen the light,
you only have two choices.
Don't look back,
walk straight into the sun . . .
or live a life
of quiet desperation.

You're strong.
You know where you belong,
but how do you get there?

All you can do
is ponder it
and stare

out the window
(far away).
A similar feeling comes over you
just like that familiar day
when all you could say
        was . . .

get me outta here
—right now.
I don't wanna be here.
Can't you see?
Isn't it clear?
I wanna be gone.

Get me outta here
—right now.
I don't wanna be here.
Can't you see?
Isn't it clear?
I wanna be gone.

I've got so much to say.
These feelings inside
keep pouring out of me.
(And although) my intentions are good,
you ignore me constantly.

I'm lonely . . .
on a cold and rainy day.
There's so much I want to share.
But all I can do
is wish for it . . .
and stare

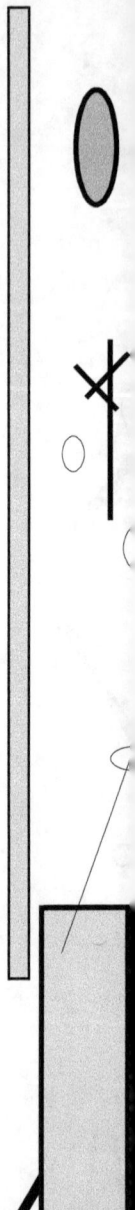

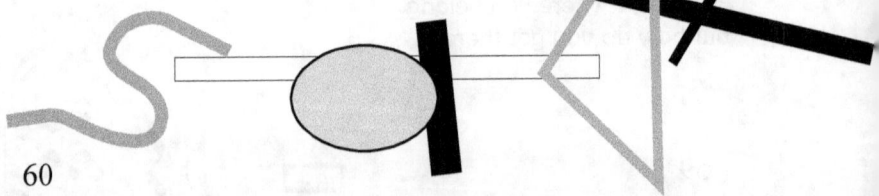

out the window
(far away)
then that familiar feeling comes over me
just like all the other days
. . . and all I can say
                is . . .

get me outta here
—right now.
I don't wanna be here.
Can't you see?
Isn't it clear?
I wanna be gone.

Get me outta here
—right now.
I don't wanna be here.
Can't you see?
Isn't it clear?
I wanna be gone.

61

Shut Down

The mind is so deceiving
when it's grieving for a loss.
Shut down is what I'm used to
and it's used to being the boss.

It gets so lonely . . .
looking for one who would love me,
truly love me;
love me as I loved you.

It's early . . .
in this morning dew
of a new life
I've found worth living;

if I can just stay in the giving,
instead of looking to receive.
When it is right,
I see the love and I believe.

Loneliness cries out—
take away the pain.
Reminding me of that tired cliché
no pain, no gain.

These feelings I've been feeling
so new, sometimes it seems,
are feelings that I used to have
only in dreams.

So I'll just go on dreaming
and you just go on leaving.

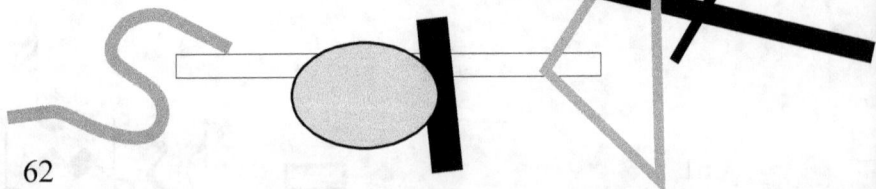

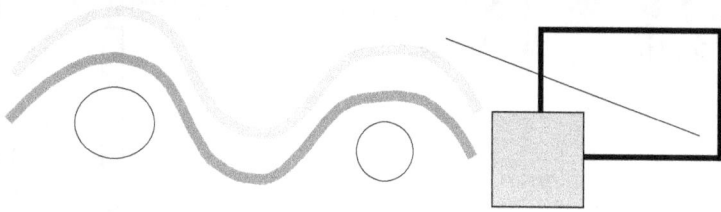

The mind is so deceiving
when it's grieving for a loss.
Shut down is what I'm used to
and it's used to being the boss.

But it's real—now
and I feel it—now
and it will be okay—now
(somehow)
because I'm right
        where I'm supposed to be
           right now!

If I Believe In You

Voices of the inner sky
calling out to me . . .
not to feel the same anymore.
Don't want to feel the shame.

The cure . . .
is willingness.
Acceptance is the key
to free what's inside of me.

Lightning strikes
in closed eyes lying awake.
For serenity's sake,
I surrender.

lonely am I.
I struggle to identify.
Sometimes I want to cry,
just need a friend.

Someone to confide in,
        I require.
Someone to believe in,
        I desire.

Could you be that someone
        for me?
I could be that someone
        for you.

Please be tender
merciful
and true
if I believe in you.

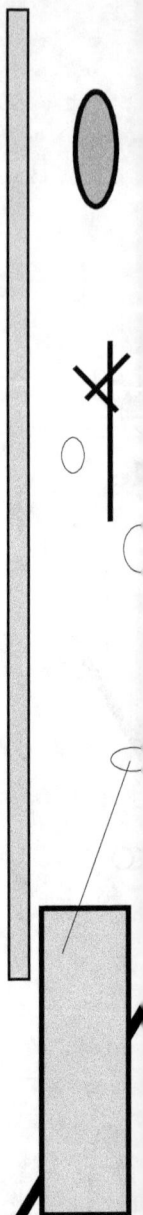

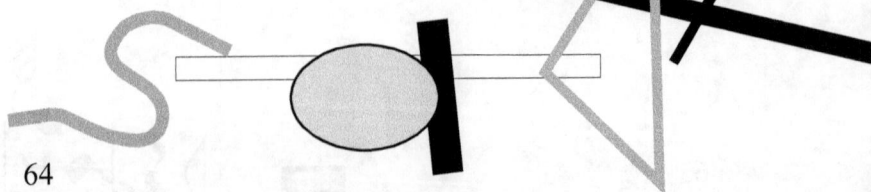

Remember,
honesty pays its own due.
It allows someone
to be honest with you.

Memory flashes
in a clear-headed mind;
speaking truth
brings trust.

Happy am I,
when you look me in the eye.
Sometimes I want to sigh,
just need a friend.

Someone to confide in,
        I conceive.
Someone to believe in,
        I believe.

I could be that someone
        for you.
Could you be that someone
        for me?

Slow Down

Slow down
>With those feelings
There's more
>You can see
Slow down
>With your thinking
In the sense
>You can be
More relaxed
>With yourself
More relaxed
>What you do
More at ease
>Feeling tranquil
With all
>Around you
Take it slow
>Be peaceful
But don't
>Be lazy
You must strive
>For yourself
And the ones
>Who are near
Make it easy
>On yourself
Or it might
>Drive you crazy
You can meditate
>Inside yourself
Your spirit
>Will be clear

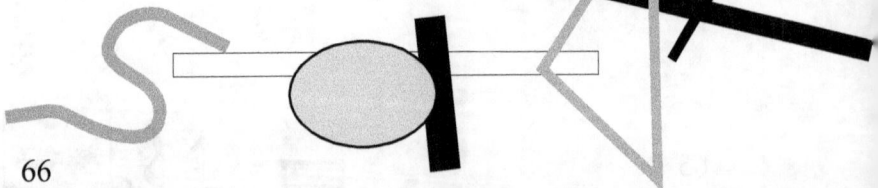

Travel Many Miles

Well what can I say?
The sun shines again today
On the sands of time,
On the way.

What a trip with friends . . .
An experience to share.
A fellowship on the river
And we were there.

Dancing and playing,
A spiritual saying
Or two . . .
And cool water blue.

What a trip . . . returning,
As if in a dream,
God gave us an adventure
To remember.

Raindrops and sunshine,
A fog bank and snow,
A sunset . . .
Like embers all aglow.

Music . . . like magic,
We sang with epic smiles.
God put on a show for us
As we traveled many miles.

So many great moments
We spent.
I am so very happy
We went.

Sing along
A happy song.
The sunlight shining
Through.

Sing along
A happy song.
You can sing it
Too.

Sing along
A happy song
Travel many
Miles.

Sing along
A happy song
Magic in our
Smiles.

~~~~

Written after returning from *The Fellowship By The River*
sober retreat in Laughlin, Nevada, at the Riverside Resort -
May, 1989, at 1 ½ years sober.

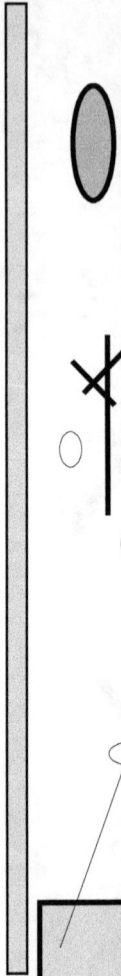

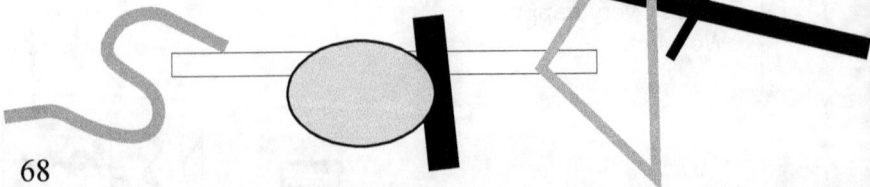

Just By The Look

They say attraction not promotion
is what keeps you coming back.
The joy you see in others
pulls you through.

And today I am remembering . . .
those words ring through (so true)
because I remember the first time
my eyes met you.

You kept me coming back.
I want you to realize
you kept me coming back
just by the look in your eyes.

Talk about attraction,
like something from a dream,
like the strength a salmon has
to swim upstream.

Like sunshine
on the mountaintop
at dusk
or morning dew.
Something like the way
I felt . . .
when I saw you.

You kept me coming back.
I want you to realize
you kept me coming back
just by the look in your eyes.

The flow of your hair . . .
it kept me there;
your smile,
all the while.

Once, at a meeting
you sat next to me.
My heart soared
over the sea.

For goodness sakes,
whatever it takes!

Anyway . . .
my attraction to you
helped me to stay.
I'm grateful!
What more can I say?

You kept me coming back.
I want you to realize
you kept me coming back
just by the look in your eyes.
~~~~~~~~~~~~~~~~~~~
Written after returning from *The Fellowship By The River*
sober retreat in Laughlin, Nevada, at the Riverside Resort -
May, 1989, at 1 ½ years sober.

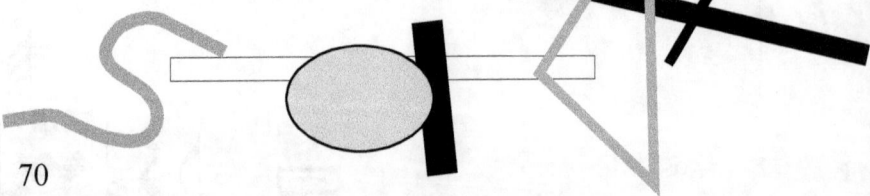

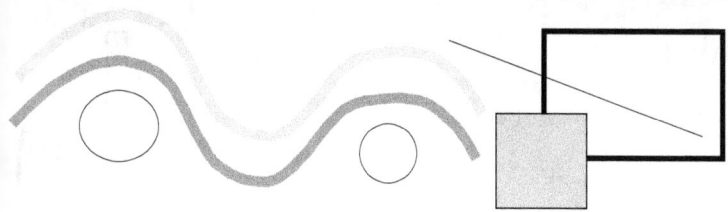

S'SSSSS

SHIMMERING

SHIVERS

SIMPLE

SENSATIONS

SIGNIFY

SERENITY

Catching Up

Many are the times I've wished
for one true friend:
someone who could help
these broken feelings mend.

And now . . .
in answer to a prayer,
I am surrounded by people
        who care.

I'd like to share with you
. . . this feeling,
that a light up ahead
is drawing near,

and the closer I get
. . . to the answer,
the more the fog
seems to clear.

It seems as though
I'm catching up
to lost dreams
(far back in my mind).

Now there is love here
to guide me.
I know I can make it
this time.

Like a raindrop,
trickling down a window pane,
leaves a water line behind it,
and the next drop to hit
that water line . . .
catches up quite quick.

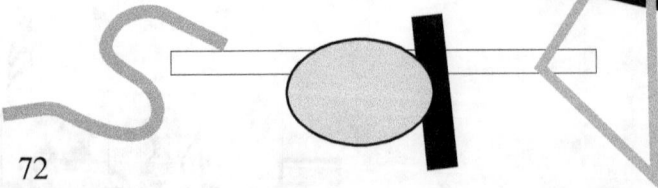

I'm catching up
to those feelings
I've left far back
in time.

A path has been laid down
before me,
I may travel
swift from behind.

I'd like to share with you
. . . this feeling,
that a light up ahead
is drawing near,

and the closer I get
. . . to the answer,
the more the fog
seems to clear.

Robin's Roost

Precision of vision
        departed;
the tension
        remembered,
not relived,
then forgotten
in the blossom of your being.

Tickled
        tenderness
                touches
                        twilight,
as fingertip
notions
encompass oceans.

Softness
        sealing;
quite
        appealing.
Feeling
        lazy,
                crazy.

Bows and bridges,
tied together
like ribbons of Robin's
        roost,
fly—   into
chronological
        consciousness.

Ring my chimes!
Hang my ornaments!
Stand in line
for perfumed adornments.

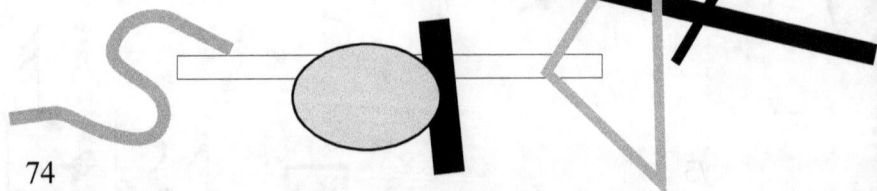

Inspiration must stay around;
for once again
        it is found.

Strength in serenity,
principles of purpose,
are directly proportionate
to the practice
        of acceptance.

A simple sign
of longitude, latitude,
        defines my gratitude.

Not only do you heal,
but you feel
        so capable
of passion's compassion.

Days later
        the answer,
(the question still retained)
for a moment
or an hour,
the alarm's time regained.

To wander
        in awe,
to wonder
        excited,
what would have been missed
had we not been
        united?

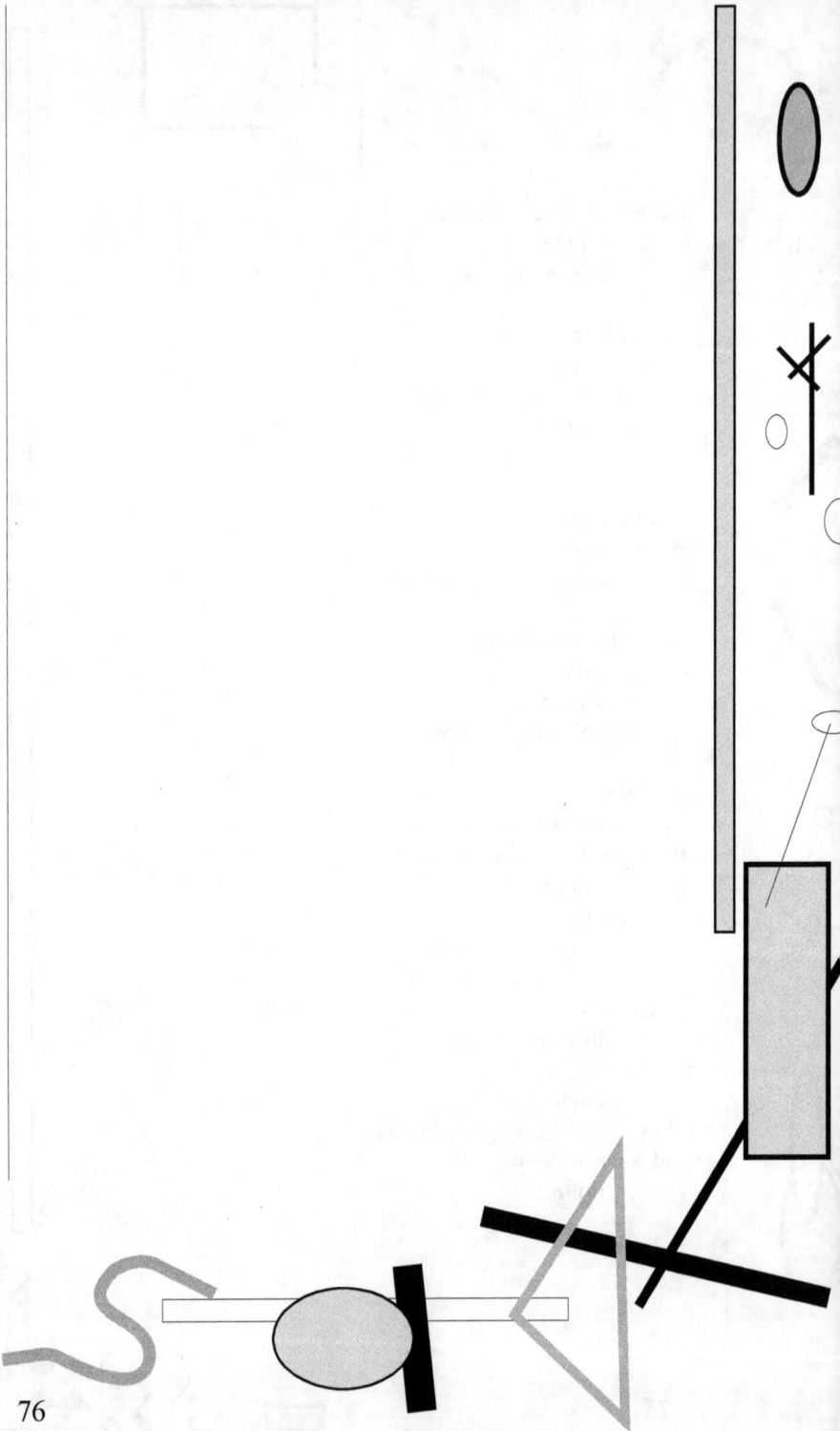

CHAPTER

5

YEAR 3:

LOOK AT ME, FINDING OUT WHO I AM

The New Frontier

Here I sit
in my wayward cubicle;
larger than some,
life just begun.

And I'm grateful for
the chance to be here;
on the verge
of a new frontier.

To go forth by choice,
not feel stuck behind walls.
The present, the future,
my destiny calls.

And I'm listening finally,
isn't it strange?
          Intuition
brings trust for the change.

While the faith that I've gathered,
in just a short time,
gives me strength as I watch
my whole life start to rhyme.

I'm excited by the prospect
of new frontiers,
after so many wasted
and lonely years.

But they weren't really wasted.
I have no regrets
because what one wants
one usually gets . . .

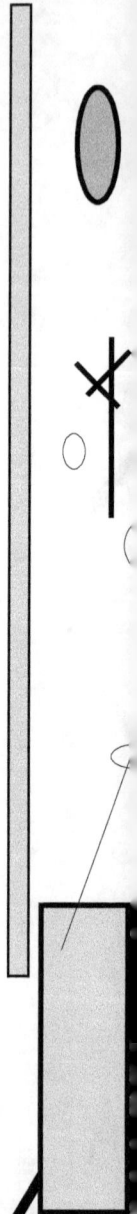

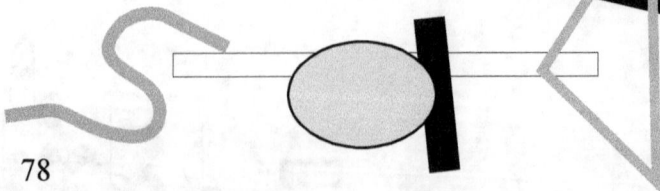

And it took all of that
to get me right here.
All I can say is
I know this quite clear.

After so many wasted
(lonely) years,
I'm heading into
new frontiers.

I'm ever so grateful
for the chance that is here.
I'm heading into
the new frontier.

The Spirit

It's more of a feeling
than a knowing:
you either get caught up
in the spirit
or you exercise your ego.

For so much of my life
my spirit has been stifled
by other people's egos,
but not any more.
The spirit is in me
and I'm not letting go.

So now I am asking
          you
to get caught up
in the spirit.
Rise with it,
flow with it,
make it your own
and take it beyond . . .
to something better.

Revel in the feeling
of participation,
tingling inspiration
and transcendence.

Get caught up
in the spirit.
Don't merely
exercise your ego.
Take it in the spirit
that it was given.

The Magic:
Ahead And Behind

1.

The curtains of the night
            unfold.
Sunshine time is here.

I wish you
were here to share
this light that shines (so clear).

Then a snowy mountain-top
makes twilight time
so bright.

I wish magic could bring you here.
If I wish hard enough . . .
it might.

The magic . . .
ahead and behind,
is what I am going to find.

2.

I do not yet own what I say,
but I am re-learning
what I have always known.

This time
I am teachable,
I know that I have grown.

Remember . . .
no matter what road
you tread,

there are always
those behind you . . .
and those ahead.

The magic . . .
ahead and behind,
is what I am going to find.

A Chance To Say Goodbye

I don't think we'd have been
so cruel to one another,
if it wasn't for the drugs and booze.
We said how we loved each other.
We tried so hard to make it work.

But we fought,
and we fought,
        oh how we fought.
How were we to know . . .
it takes a spiritual way of life
        to grow?

I think you could have been
the true love of my life
and it's not fair.

One day
you rode out of my life
on the back of a stranger's motorcycle.
I wasn't finished yet:
you never gave me a chance
        to say goodbye.

You left so fast . . .
I didn't know what hit me.
So many things left
. . . to say.

We were always fighting
that stubborn battle
that neither of us could win.
Then you rode away
in a blaze of dust . . .
and I never saw you again.

But we lived,
we lived,
     and oh how we loved.
How were we to know . . .
it takes a spiritual way of life
     to grow?

I think you could have been
the true love of my life
and it's not fair.
I wasn't finished yet:
you never gave me a chance
     to say goodbye.

Ten years later,
I'm living a spiritual way of life,
with H.P. in my heart to guide me.
I still wake up
     in the middle of the night
          dreaming of you beside me.

And I wonder . . .
     what if we . . .

But we loved,
and we loved,
     oh how we loved.
How were we to know . . .
it takes a spiritual way of life
     to grow?

I think you could have been
the true love of my life
but there was no closure.
I wasn't finished yet:
you never gave me a chance
     to say goodbye.

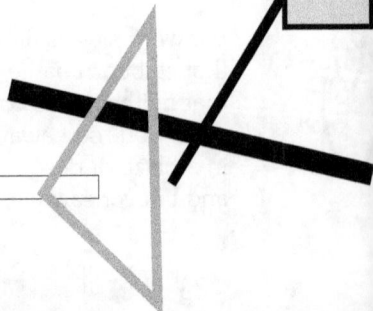

You never knew
what I was ready to ask you . . .
Just before the end,
        I was finally ready to . . .

We fought,
and we lived,
        and . . . oh how we loved.
But how were we to know . . .
it takes a spiritual way of life
        to grow?

I think you could have been
the true love of my life
and it's not fair.
I wasn't finished yet:
you never gave me a chance
        to say goodbye.

Direction Of Truth

I do not grieve for the loss
of what was
I grieve for the loss
of what could have been

but was never given the chance

it's happened
so many times before
I just don't know what to say
anymore

point me in the direction of truth

respect, compassion, consideration
hope, faith, trust,
        honesty
sensitivity to seven roots
of successful partnering

nurturing, nudging, encouraging,
trudging, sharing, daring,
declaring your freedom
to think, feel and be
        who you are

strength
        decisiveness
                security

carry on
love isn't gone
it is always there . . . to be given

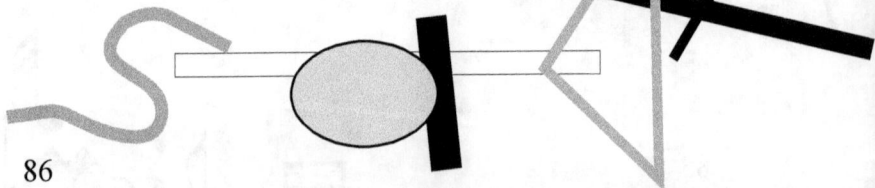

for love is not a feeling
it is an action
that produces spiritual growth
in you . . . or another

I do not grieve for the loss
of what was
I grieve for the loss
of what could have been

but was never given the chance

it's happened
so many times before
I just don't know what to say
anymore

point me in the direction of truth

87

This New Phase

Cornstalks stand there
golden brown;
having gone through all their seasons.

My life has gone through
another phase
for all the same old reasons.

But most of all
for growth,
that's what all the pain is for.

If you don't experience
the problems of humanity,
you don't know life's worth or its musical score.

It seems . . .
I'm on the verge
of something new again.

Another phase of life,
I believe,
is about to begin.

I stand at the threshold,
ready to open the door.
Once inside, who knows what I'll see.

Slowly . . . my dreams
appear more solid,
but it's not soon enough for me.

Patience is the one thing
I've always had to learn.
It's the thing that has gotten me through.

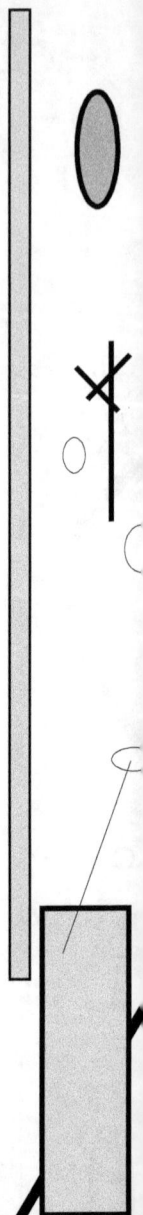

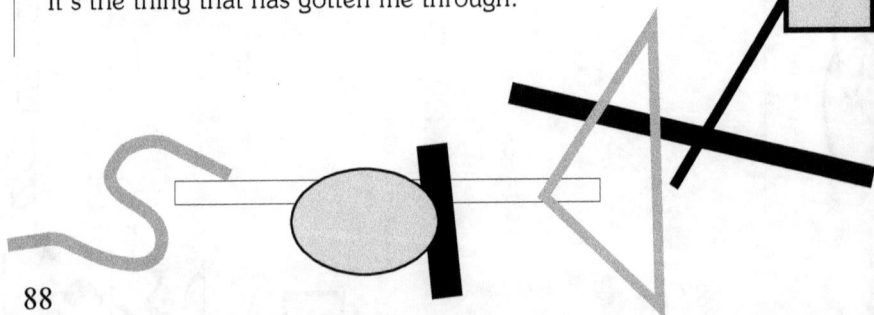

It's what keeps me going
when I think it's all over.
It's what I always come back to.

Be patient, be patient,
             be patient—
It will all come to you.

If you are living life
one day at a time,
it's going to come true.

It seems like it goes
in seven year cycles;
my life's heavy changes.

And then a major
moment happens
and everything rearranges.

And . . . boy,
it's rearranging again.
That is certainly true.

I wonder what
this new phase
is going to put me through.

Cornstalks stand there
golden brown;
having gone through all their seasons.

My life is going through
another phase
for all the brand new reasons.

Solo Journey . . . Oh

Solo journey . . . oh
The one we all must travel on
But this one is for me
The one I must journey upon

So I will journey out
Near and far to find
Where I came from
Where I'm going . . .
It's just a matter of time

Just so I remember
My journey is but mine
Your journey . . . yours
My journey . . . mine

And if our journeys touch
Then that time is our time
Solo journey . . . oh
When our journeys entwine

We came to the journey alone
And in the end
That's how we must shine
your journey . . . oh, yours
my journey . . . oh, mine

I hope . . .
At the end of my journey
I will find
The love of those
Whose journeys I've touched
            And those
Who have touched mine

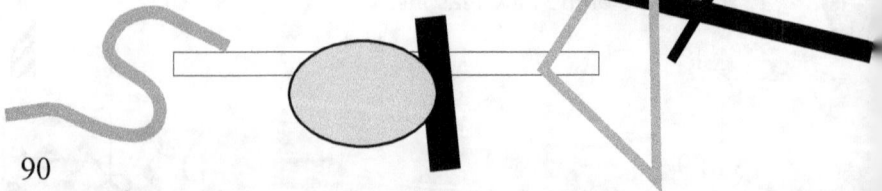

Your Wedding Day

I watched your dream
come true today.
I saw the light
that shined in your eyes.

How odd to see
we've come so far.
It's amazing
to realize.

Life gets on
so quickly:
you fix your sight
on your dreams,

then almost
before you know it,
they materialize
it seems.

Wasn't it just
yesterday
you were talking about
a life-time love,

while I was seeking
creative flair
and inspiration
from above?

And now you're walking
down the aisle,
sparkling white
like the new fallen snow,

91

and I'm writing,
playing, drawing . . .
finding that inspiration
wherever I go.

I know now it's a life
full of dreams,
that we've wanted forever
it seems;

and all we had to do
was believe
enough to take the action
and conceive

a new life
born of sobriety.

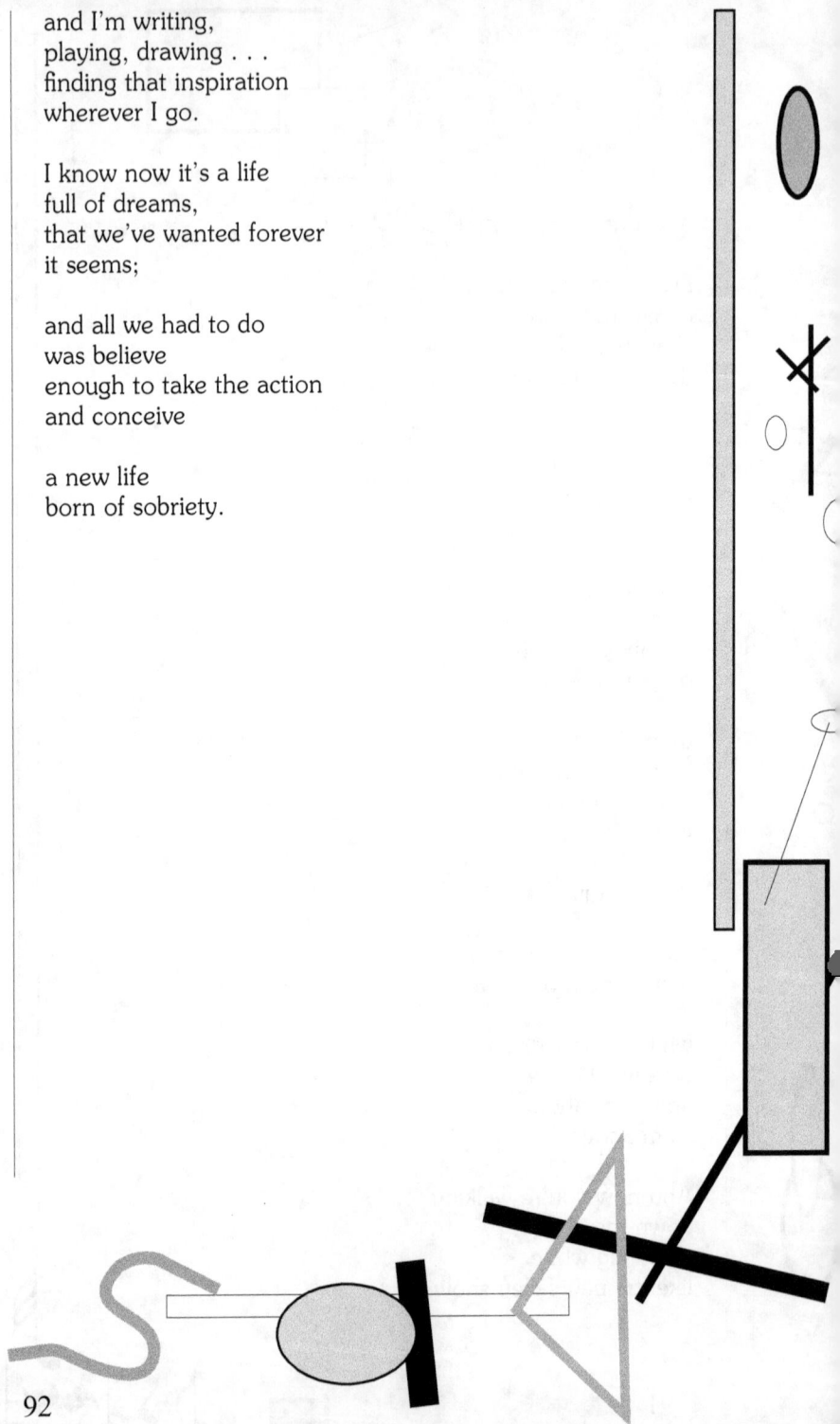

Renewal

Dewdrops are
your morning signature
gently touching
all your creations

flowers yearn
for this life-renewing moisture

I fantasize
during this quiet
morning renewal
of the moisture
the long supple kiss on loved ones lips

the soft click of high heels
coming closer
looking up
longing for that renewal

the soft knowing
of the oneness with creation

I . . .
    yearn . . .
          like the flower

Simply Satisfied

Gratefulness comes soon and quick
These days it seems
And I am full of gratitude
For the scope of my dreams

I am easily satisfied
It's not too much
It's so much
And I am simply satisfied
By your touch . . .
Your touch

I don't care what they say
Or what they think about me
For reality came back today
And paid a call you see

And I was here to participate
In the simple act of being
In the time and place
For the simple act of seeing

That I am easily satisfied
It's so much
It's not too much
I am simply satisfied
By your touch . . .
Your touch

Every day I'm grateful now
Just to be alive
For I am living on borrowed time
It's a grace to survive

And if I'm here tomorrow
It's only because of you
That I can see with clearer eyes
The sun shine through

I am easily satisfied
It's not too much
It's so much
I am simply satisfied
By your touch . . .
Your touch

Slow Sunday Start

I awake from multiple dreams:
one of fear from being chased,
one about love—a maiden from the sea,
one about work
and others as well
(more than usual).

The breeze stirs me,
clattering through the blinds.
I hear birds begin chasing the day.

I awaken further . . .
I know it won't be long
before I must rise;
another day's renewal
to ponder or act upon,
but for now I just want to yawn.

What can I say
that is interesting today?
Would you be intrigued
or even notice . . .
the stacked bricks and pine,
holding between them many musical moods:
past doo-wop classics,
rock & roll, soul,
jazz, new age
and even old 78s?

Or would the multi-coloured candles,
unused for a season on the shelf,
engage you;
as I now begin this day
            late?

And though it is bright outside
(summer finally),
I am grateful for this bit of leisure
as I wind down another week;
one of friendship stronger-bonding,
letting go of one . . .
and the painful faltering of yet another.
Also a week of irritable patience
from not smoking.

The road I'm on . . .
slow and procrastinating,
yet still ascending,
promises sweat and abundance
for another week of change
that I now leisurely arrange.

What can I say
that is meaningful today?
I'll tack it on my bulletin board
to review and remember
or better yet,
I'll set it down here,
walk out the door . . . and find . . .
today's spontaneous offerings!

Moments Of Freedom

Freedom found
In rare moments
Oh to hang onto these
I hunger

To remember them
In times of trouble
Keeps me stronger
. . . To go on a little longer

Knowing it will pass
If I just hold on

And now . . .
These moments of freedom
Come more frequent
Oh to hang onto these
I hunger

Maybe a little longer tomorrow
      I wonder
But I'm living more in today
Than in the wild-blue-yonder

And freedom found
In these frequent moments
Oh to hang on . . .
I hunger

For in these moments
      Somehow
I feel younger

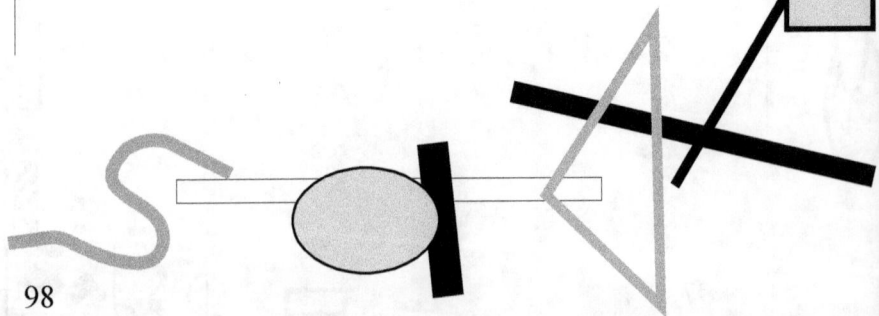

Here And There

Here
I can watch the sun
Shine all day
    There
    I'm inside and
    It's always night

Here
Everything just
Flows its own way
    There
    Whatever I say
    I can't seem to get it right

Here
I look forward to
Getting up
    There
    I can't wait
    To get away

Here
Love comes
Without a warning
    There
    Love can't find
    A place to stay
    ~
Here and there
There and here
I know which way now
The path is clear

—REVERSE

Here
I feel like I'm just watching
Pretty faces on parade
        There
        I'm watching
        Rosebuds open and bloom

Here
I feel like I'm lost
It's all a charade
        There
        Love emanates
        From all around the room

Here
I feel like I'm
Losing control
        There
        I feel like I can
        Just cut loose

Here
I feel like I
Strangle my soul
        There
        My spirit has
        Made its truce

        ~
Here and there
There and here
I know which way now
The path is clear

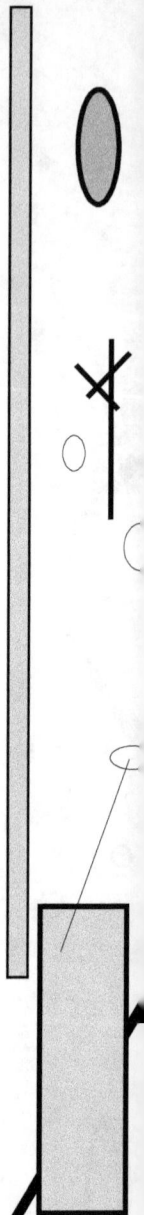

Miracle Swing

Seems like it's
A strange coincidence
What God's love
Has brought me to

Lying here
In a dream-like sequence
Half asleep
With thoughts of you

And though I feel
So restless
His plan doesn't happen
By chance

I know each rhyme
Has a reason
When I saw you
I knew at first glance

Take a ride
On a miracle train
Sing me a song
With a soft refrain

That shows me the joy
Life can bring
And swing me . . .
On a miracle swing

Everything in your time
        Not mine
Willingness to see
        The sun shine

Not blind but accepting
    The patience to be
Everything
    You want for me

Loving and free
    In eternity

. . . In this moment right now

Somehow I knew
    In a glance
God's plan doesn't happen
    By chance

Sometimes
    Makes me just
        Wanna dance

And yes . . .
It seems like a strange coincidence
What God's love
Has brought me to

Lying here
In a dream-like sequence
Half asleep
With thoughts of you

Take a ride
On a miracle train
Sing me a song
With a soft refrain

That shows me the joy
Life can bring
And swing me . . .
On a miracle swing

The essence
Of what I feel
Somehow
Doesn't quite come through

To the words
I'm writing right now
Or the paper
I'm putting them to

But if I can just express
A bit of what's in my heart
If God's plan has me here for a reason
I'm grateful that I can take part

So take a ride
On a miracle train
Sing me a song
With a soft refrain

That shows me the joy
Life can bring
Swing me . . .
On a miracle swing

Yes . . . take a ride
On Life's miracle train
Sing me the song
With the soft refrain

That shows me the harmony
Life can bring
Swing me on . . .
The miracle swing

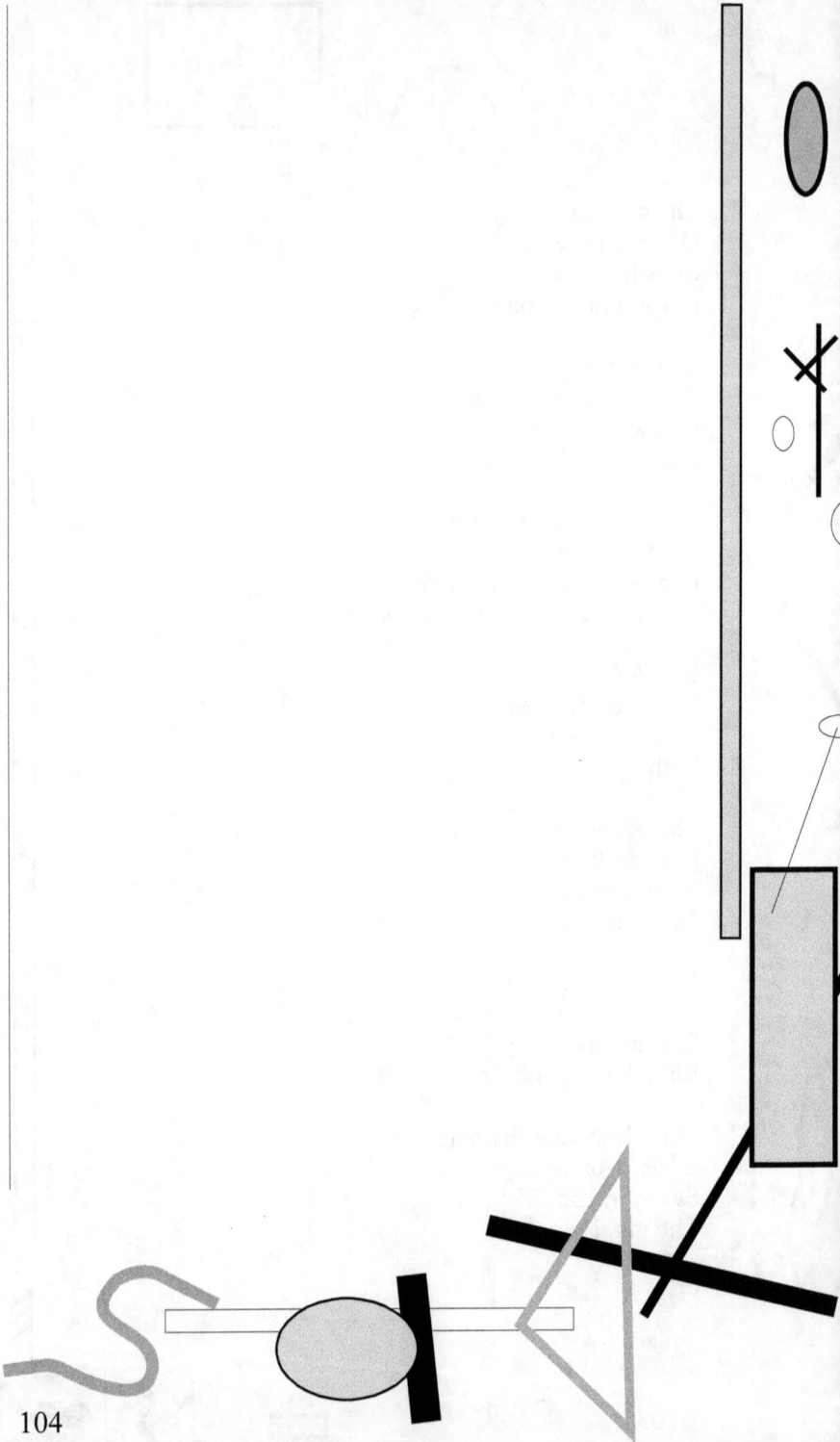

CHAPTER

6

YEAR 4:

SORTING OUT LIFE
GETTING MY PRIORITIES IN ORDER

The Magic Is Real

Oh, H.P.,
let me not forget
                the magic
that you have worked in my life.

Rather let me
remember it well,
that I may use it
as testimony.

Death was close,
knocking on my door.
That is what it took
to get me kneeling,

to pray to you. God,
to once again look for you
in my life.
To seek your help.

I prayed hard
and the very next day
you sent my friends
with your message of light

                and life.

Once again releasing me
from a long-held bondage.
A burden of ages
lifted from my shoulders.

In the wonder
and magic
of that moment,
oh, God,

true energy of life,
I knew you were real.
Help me to never forget
these moments

that I remember now,
oh God, H.P..
True energy of life.
If it be thy will.

> For I pray
> and you answer.

Conviction

I can write

About addiction

Even if I'm wrong

It's mine

And I know

Where I belong

To write

To wrong

To experiment with the song

It's quite alright

But try not to wrong

Your fellows

Right them

Send them a note

Or sing one

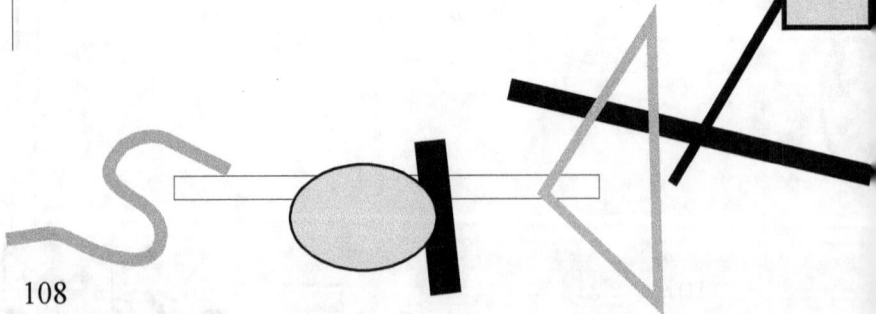

One Day

Maybe next week
you'll come back into my life
on a prayer
and a discount fare.
Try and find your way,
one day at a time.

Whether we are to be
I do not know.
I want to see you shine
in your own time.

And if that happens,
I will be overjoyed
to have helped your soul
on its journey.

One day,
just one day at a time,
you will know what love
really means.

The fulfillment of your dreams
is something I would like to see.

Maybe some day
you'll let go of that strife
you have been holding inside.

There are many friends here
to help you be strong,
while you find out
where you belong.

One day at a time.

109

When the time is right
for you and me
        to see,
we will know
what we are meant to be
in each other's lives.

One day,
just one day at a time,
you will know what love
really means.

The fulfillment of your dreams
is something I would like to see.

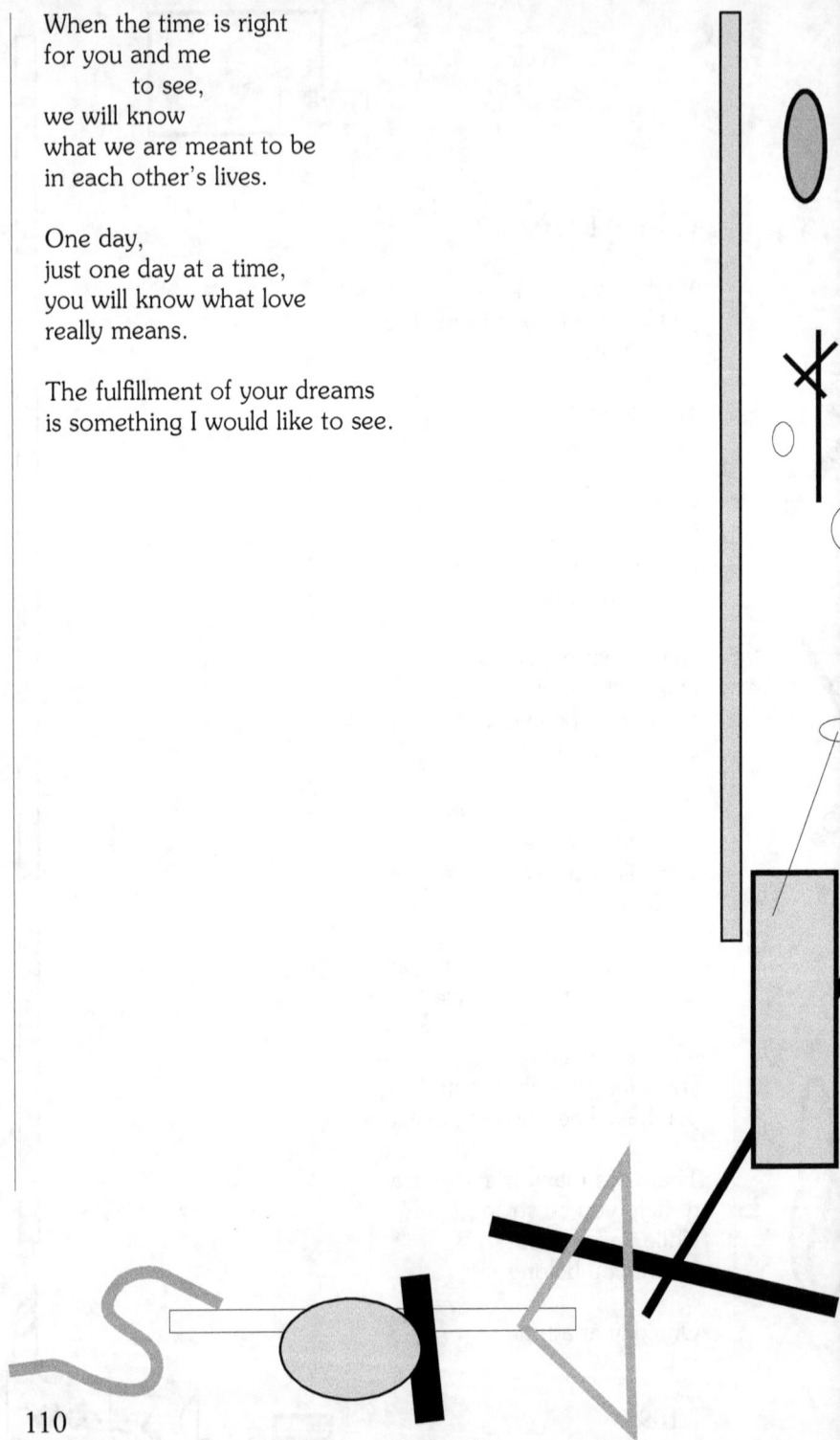

Sick & Tired

We were soul mates,
we definitely were.
You had every chance,
      but you blew it!

I got you the only free bed ever.
I even tried to help you get
      sober.
Then you threw it all away.

We could have had everything:
the child we dreamed of;
the home for the hopeless
we talked about,

but you'd rather toss your life away
to live another day
in that alcohol, pot and cocaine
      dream world.

And now you've lost everything
but the clothes on your back.
All you had—auctioned off
while you were in a drugged-out haze.

And a kindly old man
is taking care of you.
What's it gonna take
for **you** to take care of you?

Will you ever
be sick and tired
of being
sick and tired?

It's ironic. I have just finished
going through all our old poetry,
and suddenly you call after over two years,
ask if you could come stay awhile.

It's great to know
you're alive
because I've wondered—
        yes indeed!

You ask if I ever
think of you still.
You ask me if you ever hurt me.
        Don't you know?

But it doesn't matter!
It would be worth all the hurt
to see you, just once in your life,
stand on your own two feet

and be complete
—completely you,
        the **you**
that you were meant to be.

But you'll never see
until you're sick and tired
of being . . .
sick and tired.

God . . .
we were magical!
We were . . .
soul mates.

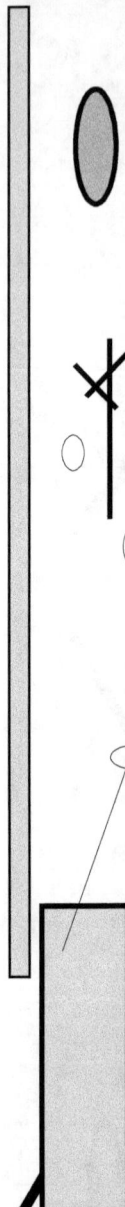

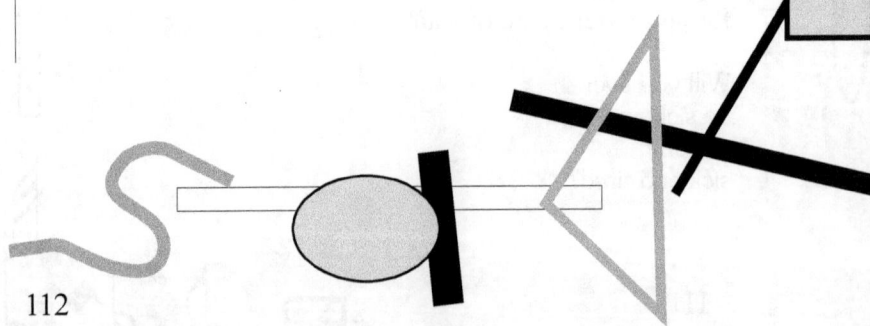

Till This One's Done

I want to finish this project
but I don't want **us** to be done;
though I'm feeling done-in
          again.

Right now I want to run and hide,
but where could I go?
Everywhere I look
It's you again.

Memories. Love lost.

Better flip the dial
on this radio, find
something calm, something soothing.
Take my mind off of me . . . and you.

But there it is . . . again,
memories of love lost.

Got to get out of myself
or get outta here,
or tear down this fence
and build a new one.

No matter where I run
I'll still be there.
Can't move on
till this one's done.

Right now I want to run and hide,
but there's nowhere to go.
Everywhere I look
it's **you** again.

Memories.

113

The Demon

There's a demon inside
That you won't let go
I want to help you drive it out
But you just won't let me know
What's buggin' you
Eating you up inside
How can anyone get through
When you continue to hide

It's a sad situation
I've got to let you go
Get on with my own life
Even though I love you so
I've tried so long to help
        Done everything
No one can make up your own mind for you
It's your song to sing

Reveal the demon inside you
Reach out and try
I'd still do anything to help you
Don't want to see you die
Only you (and God) know what's going on
And you won't let anyone in
I keep hoping to save you
I guess the demon will win

Goodbye . . . my dear old friend
Now you're gone
        You're gone
        And I'll carry on
I can't help you anymore
I can't make you grow
Even though I love you so
The demon . . . Just won't let you go

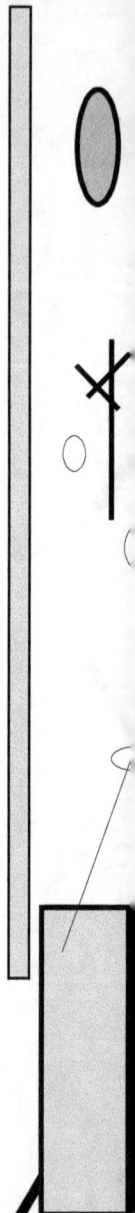

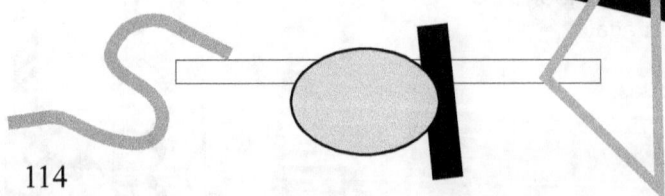

Retrieve What Is Left

remember . . .
when life was unbearable
yet you couldn't let go
> pain
> hurt
> resentments

an eternity ago
although it has been only three years
since you took the fall
and became <u>willing</u>
> to reach out
> to believe
> or at least to try
> to be teachable
> to retrieve what was left
> of a shattered life
> to be reachable

it's hard . . .
when you want to help someone
and you can't
you have to let go
let them go on hurting themselves
the only hope
that something inside will spark
to make them <u>willing</u>
> to reach out
> to believe
> or at least to try
> to be teachable
> to retrieve what is left
> of a shattered life
> to be reachable

Rest In Peace

Why is it so easy
To solve other people's problems
Yet so hard to solve your own

Take a stand . . . NOW
Live your dreams
Then see how much you've grown

Don't you know . . . anyway
Everyone in the world
Has got their own life to live

So save yourself first
Just don't stomp on others
To do it

It's hard to live
It's a mighty hard life
It's hard to give
When there's so much strife

But when it's over
You are left with you
So do what you can live with
And leave the
Rest in peace

You want to help everyone but
Neglect your own needs
You want to do what's morally right but
Fail to perceive people's greeds

Don't you know . . . anyway
Everyone in the world
Has their own karma to bear

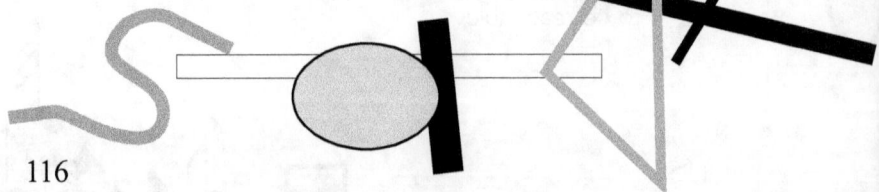

So save yourself first
Just remember to show others
You care

It's hard to live
It's a mighty hard life
It's hard to give
When there's so much strife

But when it's over
You are left with you
So do what you can live with
And leave the
Rest in peace

It's hard to live
It's a mighty hard life
It's hard to give
When there's so much strife

But when it's all over
You are left with you
So do what you can live with
And leave the
R.I.P.

117

Wisdom Of Your Ways

Although my words may seem harsh
sometimes, or angry,
they're just my feelings coming out.
I miss you.

Revenge and retribution
aren't up to me;
they are only for God.
I wish I could still see you.

But I can hear you.
I can hear you still.
I hear you.
I always will . . .

The wisdom of your ways.

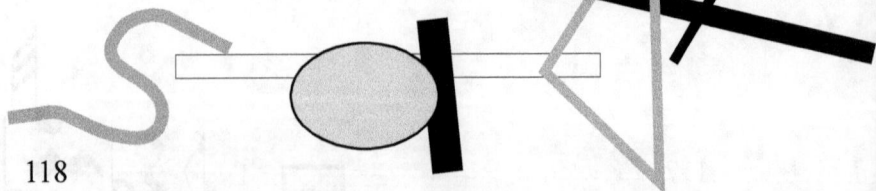

Dreams

Dreams
Dreams
How they astound me
Strange as it seems
I'm still full of dreams

As I grew older
I thought they would go away
But no, still new
The dreams
Dreams in me

Dreams

Dreams
Dreams
Today they surround me
Strange as it seems
I'm still full of dreams

119

Back To School

Knowledge
made up of
words

—wood
for building up
the fire
of that which I wish
to say

needs more tools
to build with
so off I go . . .

for sharper
instruments
to chop and gather
—wood
to build this

page

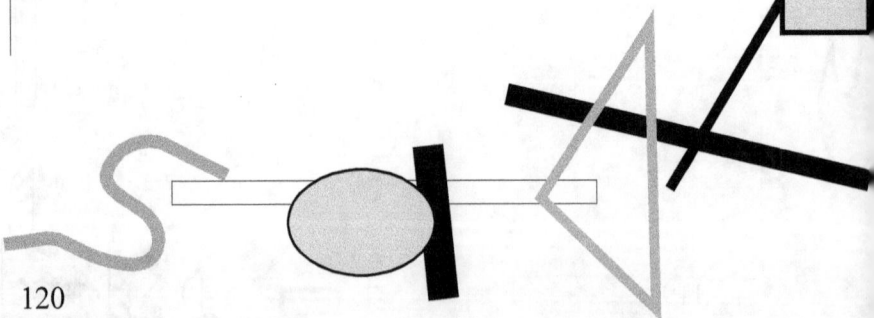

Keep Me

Growing. I want to
grow and grow and grow
in your light,
in your love,
in the path
you want me to follow.

The blessings you send
are boundless,
when I take the time
to notice.

Keep me learning about
myself and what goes on inside;
who I am and why I do what I do.

Keep fresh in my mind
that I am a student of life
and that there is no end
to my yearning.

Keep me loving,
to love others as you love me.

Let me remember
in the hard and troubling times
what I remember
so easily in the good.

Your love is all-giving, endless,
always there
by simply asking.

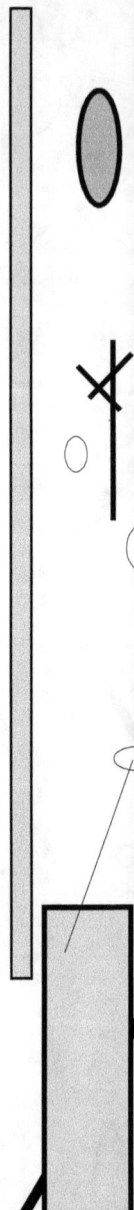

CHAPTER

7

5 TO 7 YEARS:

WITH A GOOD FOUNDATION
THE PROMISES FULFILLED

Surrender To Win

I wanted so hard
To show you
That life could be okay,

> But I didn't know
> How
> To get through to you.

I never thought
You'd find someone of your own
To see you smile.

How was I to know,
I had to let you go
To set you free?

Letting go,
Letting go,
It was the only answer.

> I had to surrender
> To win.
> Begin again.

I guess I tried to control you,
Have you do it my way.
Thought I knew so much better.

I always hoped
You'd have someone
Who would make you smile.

How was I to know,
I had to let you go
To set **me** free?

Letting go . . .

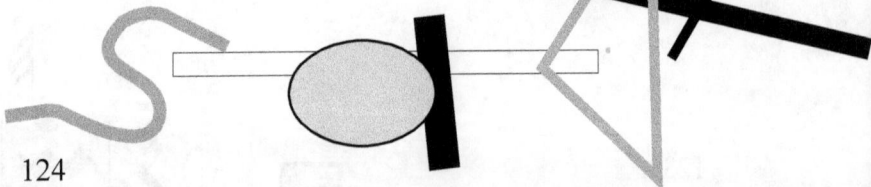

Fine-Tooth Comb

I appreciate your willingness
to help me out
even though you live miles away
I was in a rough place
and you came to my rescue
and showed me your friendship
today

it's a fine line
between happiness and sorrow
it's just one dream
from today to tomorrow
it's a fine-tooth comb
smooths your mussed up hair
it takes a friend to have a friend
show you care

And now it's just . . .
the clickety-clack
of the far away train
as I fall into the arms of sleep
my feelings shove me
right through the door
        some to let go
        some to keep

as I sum . . .
the surmountable sunrise
that's bound to shine
        in my dreams

because today you showed me
what friendship means

125

Strangers Turn To Fall

Sunshine in the springtime
Strangers turn to .

.

.
fall
Beckoned to the breaking summer
Follow true love's call

It's there for you
            For me
So much to do
            To see
True love sets you free
            Engulfs you blindly
                        Undeniably

Writing up a storm
To quench the morning
            scenery
The sheen of a song
Directs the lovers' long . . . long
            Yearning
For the knowing of the glow

        Of . . .

Sunshine in the springtime
Strangers turn to .

.

.
fall
Beckoned to the breaking summer
Follow true love's call

The Edge Of things

Here I sit
On the edge of things
Afraid to walk near the Sun
Blown by the great hand of destiny
Yearning for dreams yet begun

Out from the sky
Comes the *Blue Light of Love*
Shining like all that could be
Strikes me awake
For the first time in ages
Reminds me of what I can see

Reminds me I sing
For the ones still in cages
Convey bits and pieces
That come out in stages

And play to an audience
Fraught with despair
To shine some hope down
Through the darkness they share

I'm sitting here . . . perched
On the edge of things
You wait for me to recite
Born from the image
Of feelings I've known
Or gathered from dreams in the night

You gaze in my eyes
With the sadness of tears
For the lovers of Love
Who still fall

127

While I sing you the tales
Of the true ones in time
Who . . . knowing their fate
Still risk all

Reminds me I sing
For the ones still in cages
Convey bits and pieces
That come out in stages

And play to an audience
Fraught with despair
To shine some hope down
Through the darkness they share

Here I sit
On the edge of things
Daring to walk near the Sun
Blown by the great hand of destiny
Loving the dreams I've begun

Yes . . .
Loving the dreams I've begun

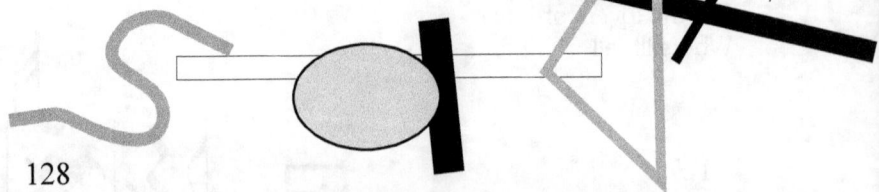

Arms Of The Present

I am by no means the judge
don't wish to be the jury
I just want to lie here in your arms

I am no longer angry
or full of fury
I am simply bedazzled by your charms

Just lying here
in the arms of the present
no longer in the past

Trying to learn
from each new moment
trying to make it last

I am not longing
to touch tomorrow
I smell the scents of today

I know that tomorrow
will be taken care of
for someone is leading the way

Just lying here
in the arms of the present
no longer in the past

Trying to learn
from each new moment
trying to make it last

129

Just Yesterday

For all the glory
And the faith
And all the time
I had to wait
For all the work
We had to do
For you to get to me
Get me to you

I am tired—elated
An appetite for kisses
But not hungry
I am full—fulfilled
From tip to toe

How was I to know
What you had in store

Yesterday
I couldn't look lovers
In the eye
Yesterday
I couldn't listen
To their sigh
Yesterday
Love songs
Made me want to cry
      Just yesterday

Now that you're here
I feel alive again
Feelings I'd forgotten
Grow stronger
      By the minute
      Hour and day
Yesterday feels so far away

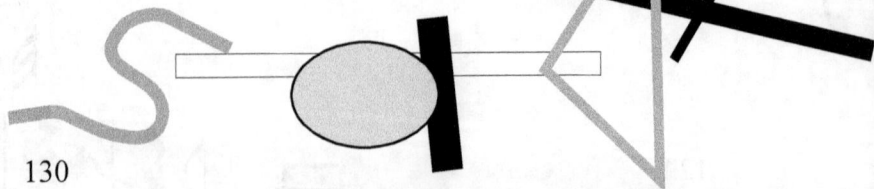

Just yesterday
I knew that I would die
Tears welled up inside
Springtime made me sigh
Yearn to roam
Like lovers do
         Yesterday

Today
The grass *is* greener
Sky bluer
Love songs soar
Just yesterday
There was no-one
But now there is
         Much more
                  Now there is you

131

Untitled

to be this calm

without a care

in our love

right now

i hear singing

in the air

singing

of silence

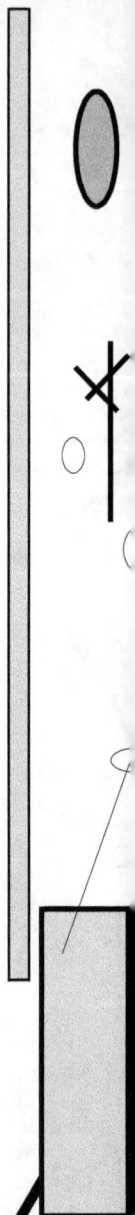
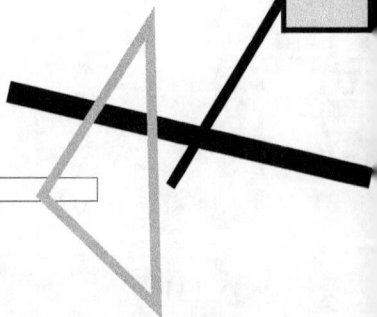

The Night
Of The Whispering Poet

1.

Scarlet sun sets
As the full moon rises
On the night of the whispering poet
Angels sing
Their song to you
Until your heart truly knows it

The Sun . . . the Moon . . . the Stars
They are my life tonight
What more do I really need
Than the Nature of God's given light

Goodnight Mr. Sunshine
See you tomorrow (I dream)
       Birds swoop and chatter
       Pelicans dive

Glowing on the ocean waves
Many share long lost sorrow
Born again tattered souls
Grateful to be alive

The scarlet sun sets
As the full moon rises
It's the night of the whispering poet
Angels whisper
Their song to you
Until your heart truly knows it

Frosty, then lacy
The water like satin
All night sound effects
Reflect my broken sleep
You run through the sand
To the brink of cool ocean
But the sand is *still* so hot
It scorches your fleeting feet

You wade into the water
So cool—your toes all tingle
Then sit in a sandcastle chair
By the waves at the edge of the sea

Shimmering children play
Present and past mingle
You stare
       Out to sea
            And you see

Party boats
Filled with prom queens
Dancing . . .
To their new found gleam

Or is it just you and me
Talking honestly
Between ice cream kisses
Floating
       On the edge
            Of our dream

The scarlet sun sets
As the full moon rises
It's the night of the whispering poet
Angels whisper
Their song to you
Until your heart truly knows it

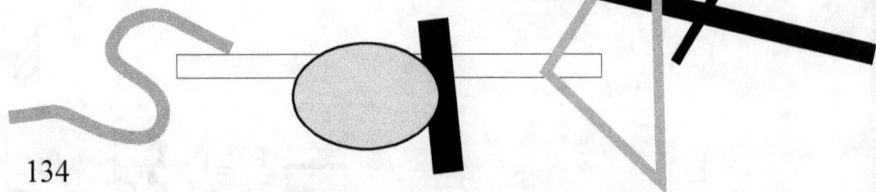

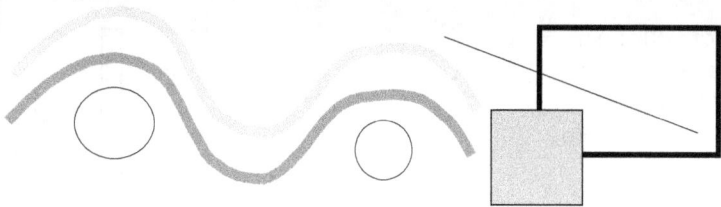

2.

The poet he whispers
Verses barely heard
Meaning profound
Don't miss a word

For if you don't catch them
You won't understand
And misconstrued nightsongs
Will be close at hand

The deeper you go
The more you will see
That this sunset . . .
And full moon
Were meant to be

The angels have flown now
Their song is long gone
Only in your heart now
They must linger on

If you remember
And if you are true
The dream we are sharing
Will follow love through
        It will be our due

On the night of the whispering poet
Your heart will know
The verses of the ages
Come down from the sages

135

The cage of your heart
Which has been closed
        Will fling open
To understand and shine

The truth will be yours
        And you will be mine

If you believe . . .

The scarlet sun sets
As the full moon rises
On the night of the whispering poet
Angels whisper
Their song to you
Until your heart truly knows it
~~~~~~~~~~~~~~~~~~~~~

A little back-story on this poem: I was living in Venice
Beach when I got sober, and for many years after. For
awhile, I lived one house back from the sand. I could see
the ocean from my bedroom balcony. One night, the sun
was setting on the eastern horizon and a full moon was
rising on the western horizon at the exact same time. The
sparse clouds created a very colorful sunset. Also, many
stars were out already. It was an astounding sight! That
night, as I slept, I dreamed about it. This poem came from
that dream.

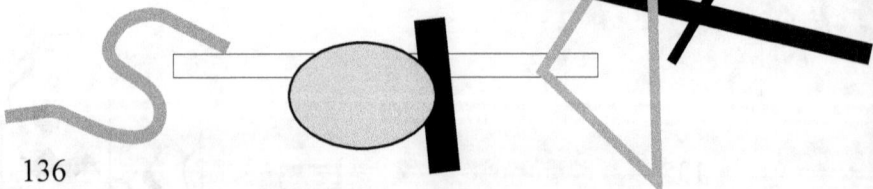

God Shot

I said that prayer for help
and the next day you answered,
        H.P.
I was intervened on,
went into a treatment center.

New Beginnings for me.
Sobriety set me free.

It was a **God Shot**
coming at me.
It just says—Gotcha.
It is something inside:

one of those little things
that I can only feel.
You do it to remind me
that your love for me is real.

I went to my first outside meeting
wondering where all the love had gone.
Hippies, brotherhood,
idealism from the '60s
—where I came from.

It seemed to have come to the meeting halls.
That night I heard my own story
told by a woman.
Her story—my story.

It was another **God Shot**
coming at me.
It just says—Gotcha.
It is something inside:

137

one of those little things
that I can only feel.
You do it to remind me
that your love for me is real.

Sitting on the boardwalk
at Venice Beach,
writing my moral inventory.
Writing about relationships,
thinking about you, Melody;
how I hadn't seen you
in over seven years
(since that day you rode out of my life
            forever).

Suddenly I look up . . .
and there you are,
—Comin' right at me!
My heart races
as you say hello,
—sinks
as you introduce
your husband.

Excited for a few brief moments,
now holding back tears.

Then you walk off down the bike path,
gone as quick as you came.
I know there is something,
more than coincidence,
brought you here . . .
after all these years.

It's another **God Shot**
coming at me.
It just says—Gotcha.
It is something inside:

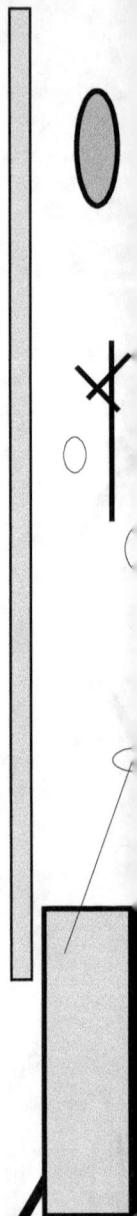

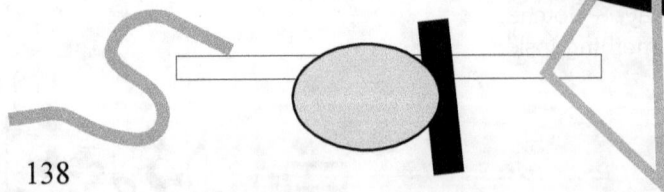

one of those little things
that I can only feel.
You do it to remind me
that your love for me is real.

And then one day,
several months later,
I'm at the movies
watching *The Butcher's Wife*,
where Demi Moore and Jeff Daniels
talk about soul mates
who were split apart
at the beginning of time;
and I know you are
that person . . . in my life,
Melody.

I walk out of the theater,
down the stairs,
and there you are . . . again,
walking up the stairs towards me.
So many things
I want to say
but your husband is with you.

You say, "How is your father?
Please thank him when you see him
for helping to bring God into my life.
I wish you God's grace."
Then you walk away.

And now it's eight years later.
I've been clean and sober for over ten years.
I've never seen you since that day at the movies

but the **God Shots** still continue
            in my life.

139

Harmony & Me

I asked H.P. in my prayers one morning,
"Why do I have so many dreams
if none of them are ever
going to come true?"

I came out of my meditation
and I was thinking about you, Harmony.
I called you up
to see how you were doing.
You said you were finally ready,
after so many years of abuse,
to pull your life together . . .
if only I would come rescue you.

So I got in my car,
drove up North,
picked you up.
You've been sober ever since.

God made one of my dreams
come true that day.
He answered my prayer.

We went out of my house
to the front yard last night,
to watch the sunset together.
You told me you had lost
your silver feather necklace
         yesterday,
in the dark vastness of my front lawn.

I happened to look down for a moment
and there was your feather, chain and all,
in front of my eyes.
It appeared as if by magic.

Looks like God answered your prayer.
I'd call it a **God Shot.**

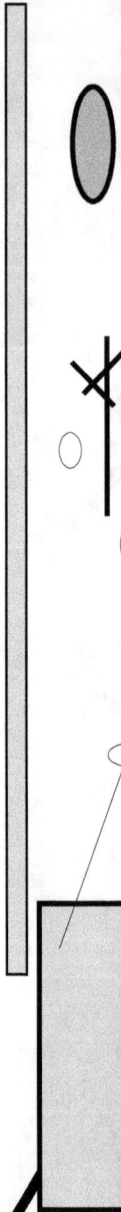

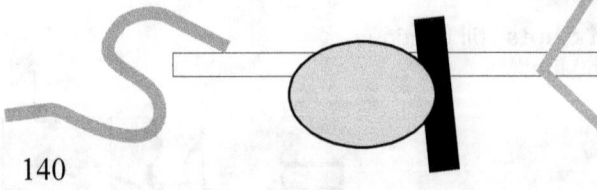

Modern Miracles

modern miracles
walk through meeting halls
grateful to be alive

sparkling eyes
sent forth to each other
for help and comfort
in times of trouble

modern miracles
brought together
by a common problem
            bonded
by a common belief

modern miracles
bringing hope
through faith and spirit

society's children
shaken and stirred
            once bereaved
            now reprieved
            live and breathe

—modern miracles

You And I

It is you . . .
who gives me gifts
lays opportunities
          in front of me.

It is I . . .
must use those gifts
take action
when the opportunities arise.

It is you . . .
molds my destiny
gives me a reason
          to be here.

It is I . . .
must have the courage
to choose my path
on this journey.

It is you . . .
who is the creator
of all there is
to be pondered, decided.

It is I . . .
must make decisions
on causes to believe in
and work for.

You . . . give me the free will to choose.

I . . . must make responsible choices.

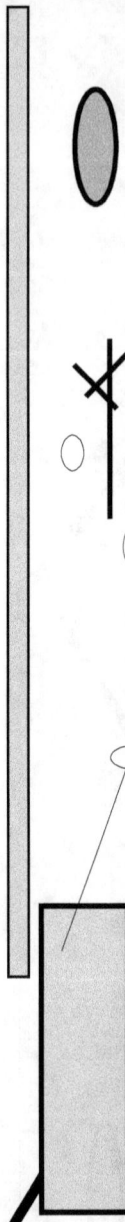

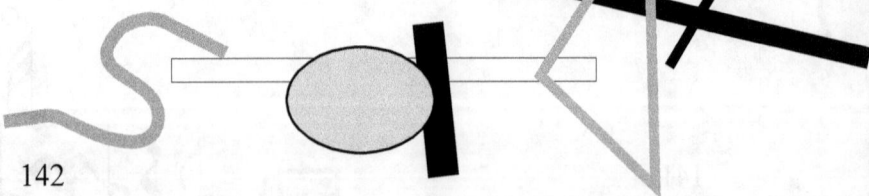

142

You Surround Me

Many birthdays have passed
since my divine awakening.
Many more to bask in the light,
to name the love surrounding,
to hold it in flight.

The words, grounded,
as if to say
the writing stops here.
Some remembered, some lost,
as I fall in and out of sleep.

The feathers—soft,
as they fall
to form the comforter:
the warm and cozy life
that encompasses me;

> to lend security, nurturing;
> the much needed reason
> I ponder the very secret
> of your season.

Too big a pile
to lumber on,
so I'll just sing the passion
of your gift as received.

—For believing is the path to recieving,
and the unused portion of faith
is never wasted.

143

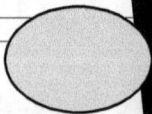

CHAPTER

8

8 TO 10 YEARS AND BEYOND:

CONTINUING ON THE ROAD TO A HAPPY DESTINY

Dawn Is Rising

Having been given
the free will of choice,
a path will be shown.
You may choose to follow,
or you may go it alone.

Having been given
a brand new voice,
a song is yours to sing.
You may choose to ignore it,
or share the joy it can bring.

Dawn is the song of today.
Sing it to me now.
Dawn is the song of tomorrow.
Far gone . . . the long time sorrow.

Dawn is rising
all around me.
In the here and now
it has found me.

Dawn is rising
on a brand new day.
I never knew it would happen
this way.

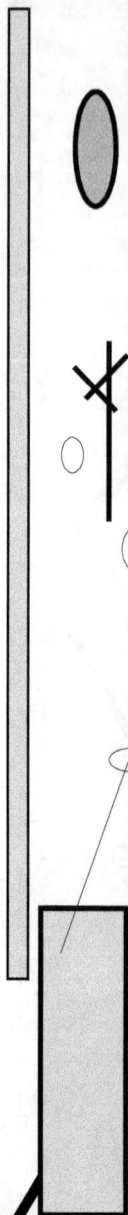

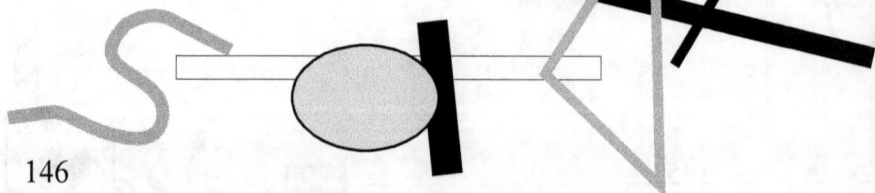

Before The Dawn Of Day

You have eluded me all my life.
I watched you pass,
my hands clasped in humble purpose.
I gazed into the blue ocean
(your eyes)
as myriad memories materialized.

I seek this moment already given.
The teacher arrives
for the student to unfold.

Just before the dawn of day,
in the light that is not
quite clear enough to see,
I see more clearly,
the future.

I dreamed I arrived in time
to see a line forming
        to wait
for what there is to know.
It burst apart as I realized
I had grown
to know what has always been known:
        acceptance is the key.

It is the dark
before the dawn.
I find my way;
the way to know
what I could never say;
the time to play
the tune I could never play

—before the dawn of day.

Emotions Looking For A Home

today I took my emotions
for a drive
they ran the spectrum

pen and paper footwork
minor details
the challenge
a good adventure entails

drove me into
an open sun-roof day
they ran down a bit
then an unexpected gift
was drawn my way
      by some news
      I passed it on

enthusiasm wore off
in a traffic jam
caught me in a time trap
looking for an off-ramp

suddenly finding them
almost out of gas
hungry as I was
keeping on the track

they searched for control
slipped through a crack
in the overflow

found their way back
the road home
enthusiasm waned
monochrome

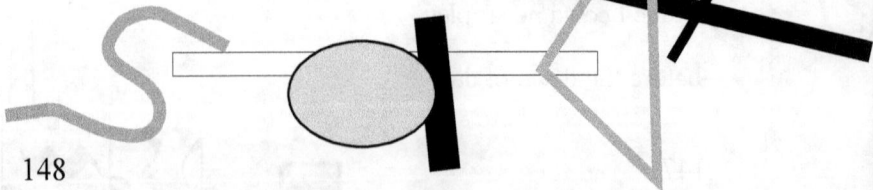

my emotions re-strained
by dingy outcomes
in the fast lane

tried to regain
inspiration
        at home
        rested
        refueled

once more
they think
I'm sinking
from the dream
I was chasing

wasn't there for me
        today

maybe tomorrow
        it will be
if emotions have their way

149

Epiphany Peaks

People come and people go
Things always change
—Ain't it so
But my soul's inner journey
Never changes
Just the scenery rearranges
As I travel to epiphany peaks

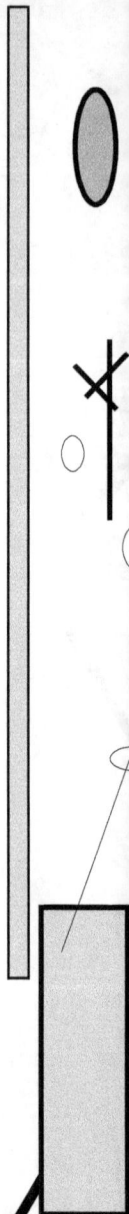

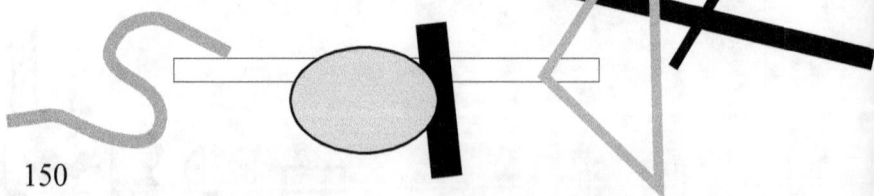

Simultaneous worlds . . . all around
Differences in peoples lives . . . abound

The rich always know
What styles and names to wear
—*Gucci . . . Armani*
They flaunt while you stare
They socialize so easily
            Carefree

While the poor struggle
            Day to day
Long hours they work
Without much pay
Live hand to mouth
—Nothing more
Trying to make ends meet
Is their daily chore

Simultaneous worlds . . . all around
Differences in peoples lives . . . astound me

People come and people go
Things always change
—Ain't it so
But my soul's inner journey
Never changes
Just the scenery rearranges
As I travel to epiphany peaks

Morning Mode

Begin my morning
with sweet nectar and a prayer.
I hear the noisy world
start to move out there.

Meditation moments
crystalize the sound.
I stretch and hit the shower.
It's a new day come around.

Another day
of magical moments;
if I can stay
in the here and now.

Show me a song to sing.
Give me some love to bring
to this new day,
    squeaky clean.

Time to see
what's out there awaiting me.
Travel down the road
in my morning mode.

151

The Way Home

you are like
an old familiar song
playing on the radio
one that soothes my soul
("*And I Love Her*")

you make me feel   .**sky**
like a comet   .*
shooting thru the . . . .*
out of control

soothe my soul
take me out of control

you are the dewdrops
when they caress the grass
the way you press your kiss
on my lips

you are like
the open highway
stretching out in front of me
on a long-awaited trip

crush my lips
take me on a trip

I'm touching the stars
and it's enough
but you keep me
wanting more

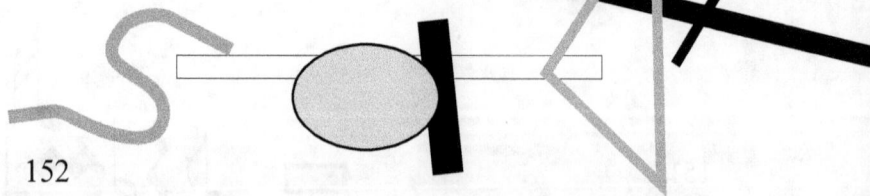

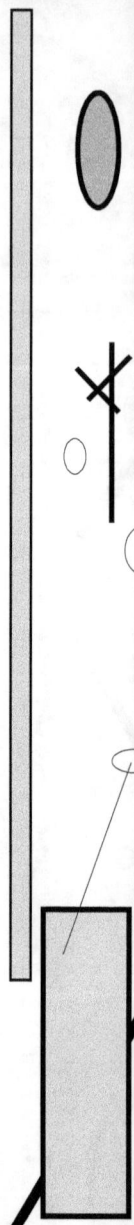

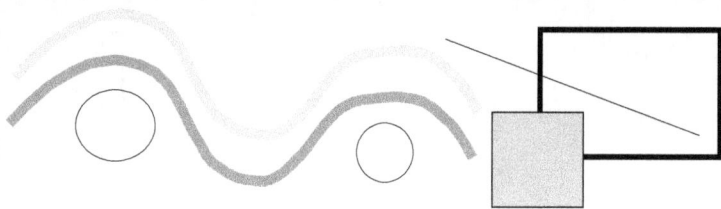

You are . . .
a sunset on the shore
with colours galore

keep me wanting more
give me magenta
  —screaming burnt orange
    —awesome baby blue

you are electric
    a heater
    warming my feet
    on a rainy day

you are the lighthouse
    in the fog
showing my lost ship
    the way

warm me
show me the way

    home

If I Could

Would I take you as I find you
Absolutely . . .
If I could

Would I build a world around you
Absolutely . . .
I would

Would it were . . .
That I could find you

Would it were . . .
My world to build

Such a thrill
I'd love you still
Absolutely . . .
If I could

If I could love you as you are
Everyday . . .
Would be just fine

If I could catch the shooting star
Its dream come true
Would make you mine

If I could sing you . . .
All my feelings
You would know I am your man

If I could wrangle . . .
All the dealings
Have you every way I can

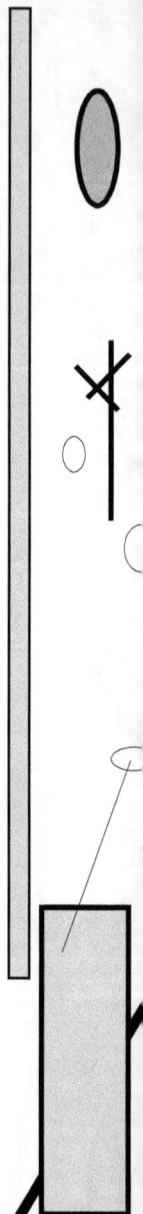

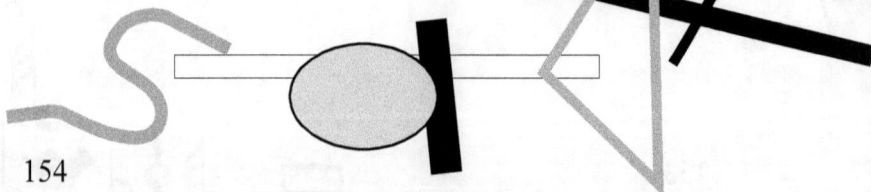

154

But darling . . .
What is true
I do have you and you have me

If you can see . . .
The way I feel
That is the way it's got to be

You know my love is real
And it's all that I can do
To show I really do belong

To you

Would I take you as I find you
Absolutely . . .
I do

I will build a world around you
Absolutely . . .
Here's to you

Would it were . . .
That you could see

Would it were . . .
Then you'd see me

And all the love I have for you
It's you and me
Absolutely . . .

If I could

Vanishing Act

Most of life is pain
With love a sweet refrain
If I could begin again
I'd still yearn for you

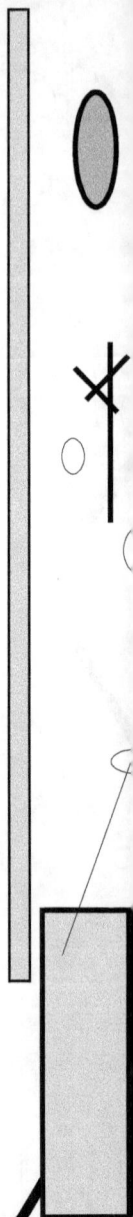

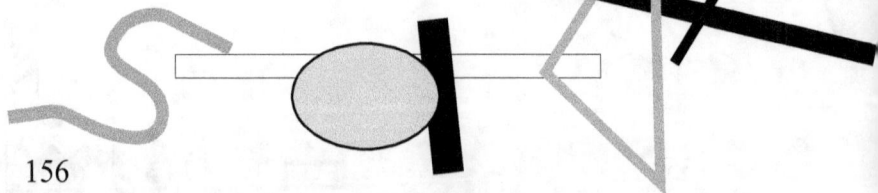

Shivering sounds of morning bring
The death of nighttime's howl
The masses gather to the highway
Another dog day prowl

If I didn't have your love My Dear
I couldn't make it through
All these things I can't abide
And all the things I do

I'm smitten by the magic call
Of music to my ear
The thunder, psychedelic Hendrix
Sounds so ultra clear

It's in me as it's always been
To help me bide my time
Foretelling our magic . . . vanishing act
From all the city grime

Most of life is pain
With love a sweet refrain
If I could begin again
I'd still yearn for you

The Twinkling Of An Eye

In shimmering pre-dawn quiet,
wedding gowns blow through my dreams.
Blue-drawn eyes on crisp new paper,
show no name . . . snowy white,
but you and family,
gathered from afar,
are quite clear.

Spare bedrooms,
cluttered with borrowed beds,
childhood laughter,
sprinkle spirit and glad tidings
for future frolic.

Love shall fill . . .
       rooms,
       hearts,
       fields and meadows!

Crystal clear,
the crisp autumn wind
blows clean the leaves
and tall grass
in the twinkling of an eye.

The awe and splendor
of colors so pure
and long forgotten,
shows sparkling in eyes
—and wonder.
Can anyone see?

Thoughts of forgotten memories
that read yet like a book
and ride on the tip of your tongue,
clear, yet fragile,
a bubble that might burst.

Write . . .
from the roots of the tree;
from knowledge started long ago.

Silence is golden
          they say.
It's more than that!
It teaches you where your heart is.
Listen and receive
the wisdom of the ages.

Walk this corridor
in the mist,
for the sake of the dearly departed;
to bring a song to life
of the old,
          of the new
                    and just started.

In shimmering pre-dawn quiet,
wedding gowns blow through my dreams.

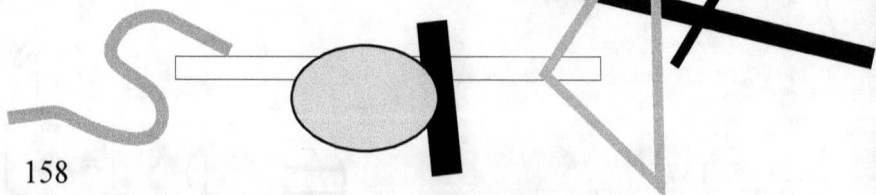

Where I Belong

This is where I belong
In this world of vivid imaginings

Forever bent on pleasing
The eyes that pleasure reading

It's the telling of my plea
That gathers in ideas gleaming

Tilled in with austere borrowing
Of words' resounding reasoning

This is where I belong
Among others like me who so encompass

Glorious dreams, inspirations
And intricate rhyme

Almost as if by accident
I stumble upon these similarities

To be and yet still to wonder
At the splendor of the artistic kind

I write so you know it is you
Who instill the insightful belonging

My pen increasingly mindful
Present in enticing serenity

Yes this is where I belong
To sing with wondrous letters

The better for knowing the realms and delights
Of fulfillment's gathering

Serendipity Sessions

In the far reaching furrows
on the frontier of the future
beyond the fear founded feelings
of failure . . .

lies this moment.

Precariously perched in the present
         am I,

and I tumble in thoughts
of the true path of passion.
Seems the fashion these days,

and I find I'm amazed
by the simplest things
that a fresh moment brings.

Can I linger here long?

May the seconds tick slowly
as I slip through the shadows
of serendipity sessions.

For the plans that are painted
on the palette of presence
are most promising
        and pure
              and profound,

and it's nice to be around.

Do I sense these sensations
for the same round of reason
that I'm writing these rhymes
to arouse you?

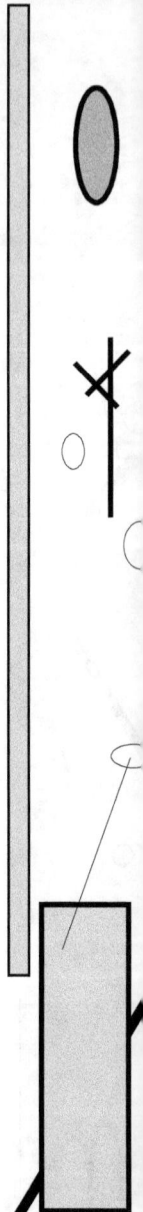

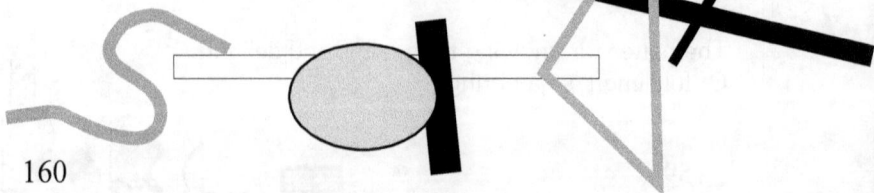

Are moments just fleeting by?

tricklings of time
I may come to . . .
      I'm here now . . .
            I pass them . . .
                  they're through.

Remember them fondly.
May they spark something new:
the next measure of moments
that surrounds you.

New Spring News

A fresh breath of air,
follows on the breeze
of night's slow dimming,
sings memories of longing
to the languid tree branches
as they sway to the music
of its invisible song.

My ears prick at particles
of soothing springtime sounds,
new again, age old friends,
inspired by the new blooming sun
of the now fading day
(that's been rained upon constantly);
welcomed sounds at last,

my heart momentarily saddens
as they pass . . .
my mind pushing forward
to night's coming pleasures,
yet hungry for the news
of tomorrow's apple blossoms.

I pause a moment longer,
        step inside
to the smell of fresh soup simmering
and running water
        singing!

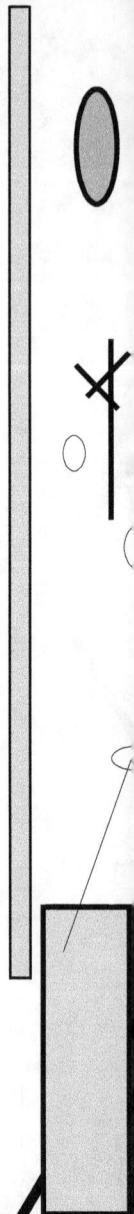

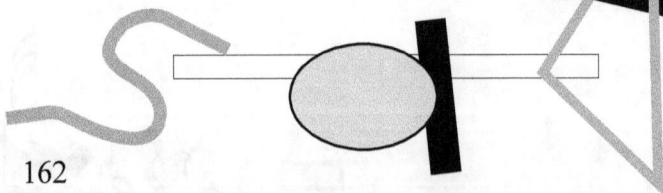

Before & After

Before
It was a struggle
After
It is the cure
Before
We worked so hard for everything
After
It is so clear

I'm here
You're here
Heading straight
Into the light
Because faith and love
Have graced us
Made us whole again

Before
We mourned our inner-child
After
Came the dawn
Before
It seemed there was such rage
After
It's mostly gone

We carry on
In our love
Our dreams dusted off
In front of us
We stand up
Walk arm in arm
Into the sun

163

THE . . .

Beginning

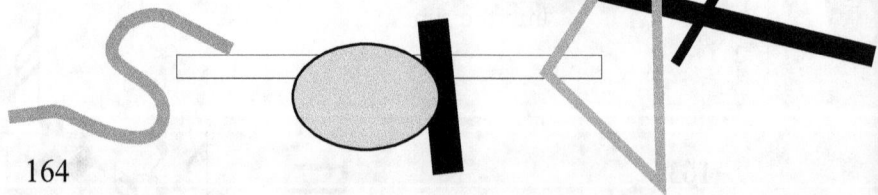

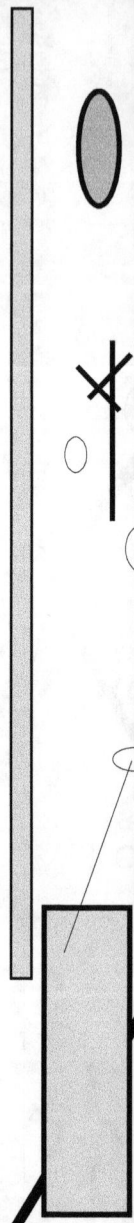

Index Of Poems

165

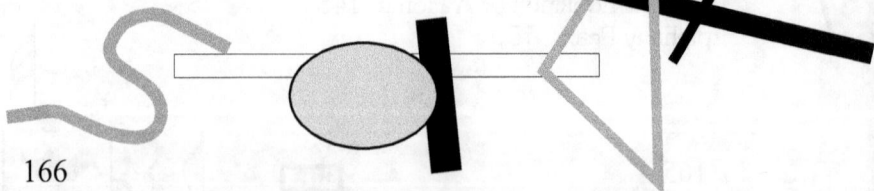

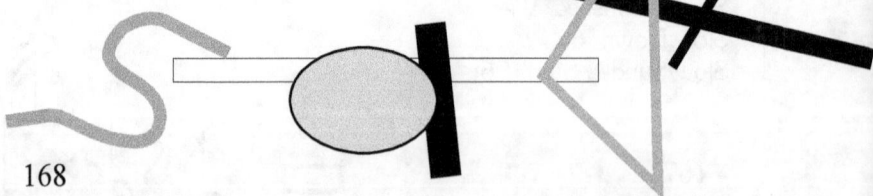

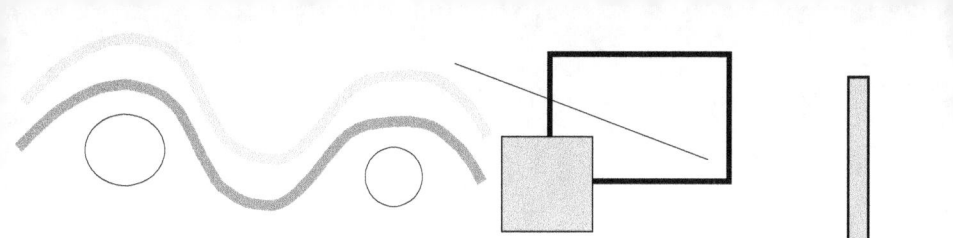

About The Symbols

PEACE BETWEEN MAN AND WOMAN: As a tribute to the 'Hippy' idealism of the '60s, Steven designed this personal symbol in 1966, at the age of 16. It is now a registered trademark. It is both a valid and timely symbol in this new millennium. For more information visit his website, www.wordsongs.com.

AQUARIUS WITH LEO RISING: Steven also designed this symbol in 1966, as his own unique signature. His Astrological sign is Aquarius with Leo rising, represented here by the Sun (Leo's ruler) rising over the symbol of Aquarius.

About The Author

C.S. Blue stands outside the normal conventions of poetry. He is a lyrical/performance poet. He reads and performs his poetry from a unique rhythmic perspective: at the crossroads of poetry and music.

Steven does not have a formal education in writing. He is a poet of the common language. He has reached many with his heartfelt words and people say it is a pleasure to read inspired poetry that they can relate to and understand. His poetry has a relevancy and honest bearing that is grounded in the current world predicament. According to Steven . . . "My poems have poured out of me since I was a boy; mostly from inspiration . . . and from dreams."

Steven is retired from a 27 year career in Stage Production in Hollwood, California. He grew up on the streets of the 1960s. Much of his writing is influenced by those sensibilities, when peace, love and brotherhood were normal, everyday topics of discourse. He has hosted readings and open mics in both California and Oregon.

C.S. Blue now pursues his lifetime calling as a lyrical/performance poet in Eugene, Oregon, where he hosts many local poetry events, including the Eugene Public Library's *Summer Reading Series Poetry Workshop and Poetry Showcase*, as well as the *Eugene Poetry Open Mic*. He publishes other peoples' work, has four published books of his own and a blog on his website, www.wordsongs.com.

www.ingramcontent.com/pod-product-compliance
Lightning Source LLC
LaVergne TN
LVHW051522080426
835509LV00017B/2169